Questions of Power

Questions of Power

The Politics of
Women's Madness Narratives

Susan J. Hubert

DELAWARE

Newark: University of Delaware Press
London: Associated University Presses

Associated University Presses
440 Forsgate Drive
Cranbury, NJ 08512

Associated University Presses
16 Barter Street
London WC1A 2AH, England

Associated University Presses
P.O. Box 338, Port Credit
Mississauga, Ontario
Canada L5G 4L8

The paper used in this publication meets the requirements of the American National Standard for Permanence of Paper for Printed Library Materials Z39.48–1984.

Library of Congress Cataloging-in-Publication Data

Hubert, Susan J.
    Questions of power : the politics of women's madness narratives / Susan J. Hubert.
        p.   cm.
    Revision of author's thesis.
    Includes bibliographical references and index.
    ISBN 0-87413-743-8
    1. Mentally ill women—United States—Biography.   2. Psychiatric hospital patients—United States—Biography.   3. Psychiatric hospitals—United States—History.   4. Literature and mental illness.   5. Mental illness in literature.   6. Women and literature.   7. Narration (Rhetoric)   I. Title.

RC451.4.W6 H83   2002
616.89'0082—dc21   2001053467

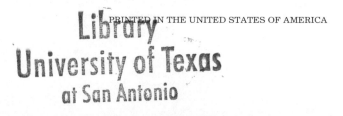

To the memory of my mother

Contents

Acknowledgments

Numerous people helped to bring this project to completion, both in its present form and in its preliminary version as my doctoral dissertation. First, I would like to acknowledge the mentoring and encouragement provided by my dissertation director, Gwendolyn Etter-Lewis, and my committee members, John Saillant, Jil Larson, and Tracey Mabrey. In addition, many colleagues, friends, and family members also supported my work or otherwise contributed to this project, and I would particularly like to thank Gwen Raaberg, Arnie Johnston, Rosalyn Reeder, Scannell McCormick, and Debbie Renard. Finally, I would like to thank the University of Delaware Press and Associated University Presses.

Questions of Power originated during a particularly difficult time in my life. My mother and father died shortly before I began considering dissertation topics, and I put my studies aside to deal with the personal and practical ramifications of my loss. While sorting through more than a lifetime's accumulation of personal belongings, I came upon an old calendar with handwriting on the back of several pages. For reasons beyond my awareness, I was moved to read the words aloud, and I soon realized that I was reading my maternal grandmother's reflections on her life. My grandmother had died before I was born, but I felt that I had finally met her through the experience of reading her handwriting and hearing her words in my voice.

Surely my grandmother's writing moved me because she was my mother's mother, even though she was both kin and stranger to me. Yet, the poignancy of discovering my grandmother's life writing caused me to realize that I could, in a sense, "meet" other people by reading and studying autobiographies. My study of the narratives for this project was at times nearly as meaningful to me as reading the words of my grandmother. There is much to admire in lives of the women who wrote these narratives and much to be moved by in their stories. I am proud to claim these women as my "unrelated kin."

11

Questions of Power

1

Women's Madness Narratives and the Sentence of History

In *THE LOCATION OF CULTURE*, HOMI BHABHA WRITES, "A RANGE of contemporary critical theories suggest that it is from those who have suffered the sentence of history—subjugation, domination, diaspora, displacement—that we learn our most enduring lessons for living and thinking."[1] By analyzing autobiographical writing by women who were treated for psychiatric problems, the present study focuses on women who suffered and confronted the sentence of history. Elizabeth Packard, Ada Metcalf, Clarissa Lathrop, and Lydia Smith claimed that they were falsely labeled as insane and unjustly incarcerated in asylums. Other women, such as Jane Hillyer, Barbara Field Benziger, and Joanne Greenberg, viewed their suffering primarily in terms of the ravages of mental illness. Writers such as Kate Millett, Jill Johnston, and Susanna Kaysen are critical of psychiatric and cultural understandings of "mental illness."[2] Although they understood the cause of their suffering in different ways, all of these women confronted the sentence of history through autobiographical writing.

An analysis of these autobiographical accounts necessarily engages scholarship in several areas, including medical and social history, psychiatry, and feminist theory, as well as literary and cultural analysis of the texts themselves. Autobiographical writings by mental patients have come to be seen as important sources for the history of psychiatry. Similarly, feminist scholars have turned to women's autobiographies for evidence of gender bias in psychiatric practice and cultural attitudes about women. The emphasis of the present study, however, is neither historical nor theoretical; the main focus is on the lives of the women themselves. Yet, it is important to ask what these

narratives can teach us—not only about madness and its treatment, but also about life and living. The underlying premise of
this study is that we have much to learn from the narratives of
women who confronted their experiences of madness and psychiatric treatment through autobiographical writing.

First-person accounts of psychiatric treatment constitute a
largely untapped set of sources for historians of psychiatry.[3] In
their edition of selections from women's asylum autobiographies, Jeffrey Geller and Maxine Harris assert that autobiographical accounts present a missing part of the history of
psychiatry.[4] Roy Porter argues for the necessity of writing
medical history from the patient's point of view, which he
refers to as a "sufferers' history of medicine."[5] Traditional histories of psychiatry—and, ironically, their radical counter-
parts—imply that "the history of medicine is about doctors,
what they know, what they do."[6] According to Porter, physician-centered accounts of the history of medicine may involve
"a major historical distortion."[7] First-person accounts are
therefore essential to the historical enterprise. By ignoring the
sufferers' role in the history of healing, historians have presented an incomplete and potentially inaccurate picture.
Moreover, Porter writes, "A people's history of suffering might
restore to the history of medicine its human face."[8]

As Geller and Harris point out, psychiatric history has been
written from the perspective of those with institutional
power.[9] According to Porter, "One function—or at least by-
product—of the rise of institutional psychiatry and psychiatric
theory has been a habit of not listening to the mad."[10] Most of
the early histories of psychiatry were written by psychiatrists
themselves. Traditionally, the history of psychiatry has been
understood as a triumph of science and humanitarianism over
ignorance and superstition. These "Whig" histories recount the
progressive development of psychiatry, in which the care of the
mentally ill is enhanced by steady advances in medical science.[11]

Whig historiography dominated the field in the 1930s, 1940s,
and 1950s, although Albert Deutsch's sociological study, *The
Mentally Ill in America*, is a notable exception.[12] The 1960s
marked the beginning of the era of alternative histories and the
movement of antipsychiatry. Social historians, such as Michel
Foucault, David Rothman, and Andrew Scull, presented a rad-

ically different image of the rise of psychiatry.[13] To group these historians together is misleading, as their perspectives differ on crucial points; however, they are all associated with the notion that, far from being a benevolent institution, psychiatry functions as a powerful agent of social control.[14] At approximately the same time that historians were offering radical alternatives to the standard histories of psychiatry, antipsychiatrists were interrogating the very nature of psychiatric practice. Antipsychiatrists, most notably R. D. Laing, David Cooper, and Thomas Szasz, not only explicated the social conformist elements of psychiatric practice but also questioned biological bases for "mental illness." [15] Erving Goffman's *Asylums*, a sociological study, contributed to the critique of psychiatry by arguing that mental hospitals function more as institutions of social control than as medical treatment centers.[16] The work of Goffman and the antipsychiatrists also served to problematize the views of previous histories of psychiatry.

However, neither the radical historians nor the antipsychiatrists paid particular attention to the role of gender in psychiatric practice. Second-wave feminists, on the other hand, were quick to make connections between sexism and psychopathology, and psychiatry was among the first institutions critiqued by feminists in the 1970s.[17] Kate Millett and Shulamith Firestone articulated the misogynist underpinnings of psychoanalysis, and Phyllis Chesler's *Women and Madness*, published in 1972, quickly became a landmark work in feminist approaches to "mental illness."[18] Chesler documented the "double standard of mental health," which is interwoven into the structures of patriarchal dominance.[19] Women "are categorically denied the experience of cultural supremacy, humanity, and renewal based on their sexual identity," she writes. "In different ways, some women are driven mad by this fact."[20] Chesler's condemnation of psychiatric practice also contributed to the development of feminist approaches to psychotherapy.[21]

Feminists have also contributed to the ongoing work in the cultural history of psychiatry. Elaine Showalter's *The Female Malady* analyzes the relationship of psychiatry to the wider culture and argues that madness is a gendered category.[22] By focusing on English culture, Showalter explores the ways that "women" and "madness" have been associated in medical and literary discourse. Other feminist literary scholars turned their attention to the relationship between madness and writing, either in actuality or symbolically. In *The Madwoman in the Attic*, Sandra Gilbert and Susan Gubar see the mad woman as an apt symbol for the woman writer; however, as Maria Caminero-Santangelo points out, Gilbert and Gubar do not fully address the place of the mad woman in society.[23] In *The Mad Woman Can't Speak*, Caminero-Santangelo begins her exploration—and rejection—of the use of madness as a metaphor by examining autobiographical accounts written by so-called mad women. Mary Elene Wood's *The Writing on the Wall*, on the other hand, primarily analyzes first-person accounts of psychiatric treatment instead of literary works. Wood offers a feminist perspective on several important narratives by American women.[24]

Critics of the psychiatric system have taken their place alongside the work of Foucault, Laing, and Chesler. As this study will show, patient accounts of psychiatric abuse are nothing new. According to Norman Dain, "The most persistent critics of psychiatry have always been former mental hospital patients."[25] Yet, as Dain points out, a significant ex-patient movement emerged in the 1970s and 1980s, partly because of the influence of antipsychiatry, and first-person accounts of psychiatric abuse played a prominent role in this movement.[26] The interest in the narratives of mental patients, which was sparked by the ex-patient movement and the work of such writers as Foucault, Laing, and Chesler, also led to the publication of selections from previous first-person accounts of psychiatric patients.[27] The link between the theoretical work of the era and autobiography is apparent in Chesler's statement that *Women of the Asylum*, an anthology of firsthand accounts of psychiatric treatment, is a "companion volume" to her *Women and Madness*.[28]

The present study differs from previous work in women's autobiographies by focusing on what I have chosen to call "madness narratives." Although I am not the first to use this term, I am not aware of any previous attempts to define it theoretically. As a theoretical construct, the concept of the madness narrative extends the limits imposed by traditional definitions of autobiography in relation to accounts of psychiatric treatment. In *The Writing on the Wall*, Wood largely restricts her discussion to "asylum autobiographies," a term that reflects her interest in "how a woman institutionalized as insane structured a narrative for public consumption."[29] In general, she follows Estelle C. Jelinek's definition of autobiography as "that work each autobiographer writes with the intention of its being her life story—whatever form, content, or style it takes."[30] Although Jelinek writes that the genre of autobiography defies formal definition, she eliminates journals, diaries, and letters from the genre.

My use of the term "madness narrative" is designed to be more inclusive than Wood's category of asylum autobiography or Jelinek's definition of autobiography as a genre. I have chosen a more inclusive term because the insistence that autobiographies must be intentionally presented as life stories does not take into consideration the stigmatization, which continues even after recovery, of individuals who have been labeled "mentally ill." Regardless of whether they were forcibly incarcerated or voluntarily agreed to treatment, writers may choose to present their experiences pseudonymously or in the guise of fiction. The term "madness narrative" includes novels, journals, anonymous accounts, and narratives presented by an interlocutor, as well as traditional autobiographies. Also, the designation avoids the boundaries of asylum autobiography and therefore allows for the consideration of madness narratives that are not centered on the experience of hospitalization. I define madness narrative as a firsthand account of the experience of "mental illness" and psychiatric treatment, even if the narrative is presented as a fictitious account or case study.

As Porter states, "The history of madness is the history of power."[31] Indeed, by analyzing the questions of power that underlie women's madness narratives, I am focusing on the political aspects of psychiatric treatment rather than the experience of "mental illness." My discussion of the "politics" of women's madness narratives follows Kate Millett, who uses *politics* to refer to "power-structured relationships, arrangements whereby one group of persons is controlled by another."[32] In using the word *madness*, I am drawing on the work of theoreticians such as Michel Foucault and Jane Ussher. According to Ussher,

To use the term "madness" is to recognize the meaning attached to the perception of illness or dysfunction in the psychological domain—the stigma attached—and to avoid entering into the discourse of the experts wherein these different classificatory systems are deemed to exist as entities in themselves, as illnesses which *cause* the disturbance in function in the first place.[33]

The avoidance of psychiatric jargon or common labels such as "mental illness," "crazy," and "insane" serves as a linguistic way of questioning the easy adoption of psychiatric concepts of mental disease. I make no attempt to diagnose the women whose work is analyzed in this study. The designation of "madness narratives"—as opposed to "accounts by mentally ill persons"—reflects my desire to interrogate the discourses that maintain the social construction of mental illness and the bifurcation of sanity and insanity.

In problematizing mental illness as a category of disease, I have turned in particular to the work of Foucault and the intellectual leaders of the antipsychiatry movement, particularly Laing and Szasz. Foucault, Laing, and Szasz, among others, have contributed not only to an analysis of what is meant by "mental illness" but have also explicated the policing function of psychiatric diagnoses. Foucault focuses on the genealogy of the discourse of madness, and his work analyzes the structures of power inherent in these discourses. Laing, Cooper, and Szasz not only reject the medical model of "mental illness" but also question the whole notion of mental illness. In his early work, Laing attributes the problems experienced by individuals to a "sick" society. For Laing, madness is a sane response to an insane society. According to Szasz, mental illness is a "myth" and psychiatric diagnoses are reified concepts invented to explain as well as label behavior that violates social codes. These analyses of the social construction of madness and the enforcement of an often dull conformity have led to a reassessment of psychiatric treatment and to understandings of the mind that transcend such designations as sanity and insanity.

The work of psychiatrist Frantz Fanon, whose theoretical writings address the psychological impact of racism and colonialism, provides an important link between madness and oppressive social structures.[34] Fanon's insights about the psychological effects of subjugation are particularly important in my consideration of the madness narratives of African writer Bessie Head. At the same time, Fanon's articulation of the link between madness and subjugation can also be applied to the psychological oppression of women in patriarchal societies. In *Black Skin, White Masks*, Fanon presents evidence that Euro-Americans treat Africans as subhuman, primitive, or, at best, mentally deficient in comparison to whites. The psychological consequences of racial oppression can include a profound personal and communal alienation, sometimes resulting in a desire to be "white." As Fanon writes,

> I begin to suffer from not being a white man to the degree that the white man imposes discrimination on me, makes me a colonized native, robs me of all worth, all individuality, tells me that I am a parasite on the world, that I must bring myself as quickly as possible into step with the white world.[35]

Similarly, women who wish to be taken seriously as artists or intellectuals sometimes adopt a "male" pose. However, just as a mask does not change the color of one's skin, women cannot "become" men. Moreover, individuals who fail to adhere to the limits imposed by society on account of their race, sex, or social class risk annihilation, including the annihilation of the self through psychiatric incarceration.

Despite the importance of the work of Foucault, Laing, and Fanon, I am reluctant to read women's lives exclusively through the framework provided by male theoreticians. The majority of male writers have failed to address the role of gender in psychiatric diagnosis and confinement, and feminist analyses offer an important corrective to androcentric studies. Showalter, for instance, criticizes the British antipsychiatry movement for its androcentric bias (although much of her discussion focuses on the therapeutic practices of Laing and Cooper rather than the significance of their theories). Moreover, as feminist theoreticians have pointed out, women learn to see themselves through masculine eyes.[36] Placing women's narratives at the center of my study necessarily involves an engagement with the work of scholars who have continued the ongoing analysis of the role of gender in psychiatric diagnosis and treatment.

Jane Ussher's work is particularly relevant to my study of madness narratives because of her assessment of the various critiques of psychiatric practice. While accepting the valid criticisms of Laing, she resists the tendency of his theories to romanticize madness. According to Ussher, even feminists have presented an incomplete analysis of women's madness. She writes,

> Madness is more than a hormonal imbalance, a set of negative cognitions, a reaction to a difficult social situation, or the reflection of underlying unconscious conflict. Madness is more than a label. It is more than a protest. It is more than a representation of women's secondary status with a phallocentric discourse, a reaction to misogyny and patriarchal oppression. To understand madness we must look further and wider than the individual to the whole discourse which regulates "women." Yet we must also look beyond the category of "women" to the reality of the pain and desperation which is a part of this experience for the individual in distress.[37]

Ussher cautions us that we should not lose sight of the women at the heart of the debates about madness. Although we need to understand the societal implications of "madness," our explanations cannot ignore the real suffering experienced by those who are perceived to be mad. "As women," Ussher writes, "we are regulated through the discourse of madness. But the woman herself is real, as is her pain—we must not deny that. So we must listen to women."[38]

I strongly agree with Ussher's insistence on listening to women. For this reason, the most important theoretical consideration for me goes beyond a preference for feminist analyses written by women scholars. The particular value of madness narratives is that they allow us to listen to the voices of "mad" women. As Leslie Rebecca Bloom writes,

> One of the purposes of examining subjectivity in women's personal narratives is to redefine what it means for women to write, tell, discuss, and analyze their life experiences against the backdrop of the prevailing discourses that seek to silence them. To change the master script is to change reality; to change reality is to participate in making a history different from the one the status quo would produce.[39]

My primary method has been to listen to these stories with an openness to the women's own understandings of their circumstances and to interpret their narratives both critically and sympathetically.

By placing women's madness narratives at the heart of my study, I intend to articulate the theories that are already present in the women's stories rather than apply theoretical constructs to their narratives. Barbara Christian argues that, as a result of the dominance of "theory" in literary studies, "some of our most daring and potentially radical critics (and by *our* I mean black, women, third world) have been influenced, even coopted, into speaking a language and defining their discussion in terms alien to and opposed to our needs and orientation."[40] Christian also points out that there are more ways to understand "theory" than the way that it is typically discussed among literary critics today. Christian writes that the theorizing of people of color, particularly women of color,

> is often in narrative forms, in the stories we create, in riddles and proverbs, in the play with language, since dynamic rather than fixed ideas seem more to our liking. . . . And women . . . continuously speculated about the nature of life through pithy language that unmasked the power relations of their world.[41]

Following Christian, I strive to let the work itself, rather than particular theoretical frameworks, determine my approach.

The majority of the narratives that I consider were written by American women, but I have included a discussion of works that go beyond the limits of American studies. My rationale for including a chapter on Janet Frame's autobiography and Bessie Head's *A Question of Power*, other than the significance of the works themselves, is multifaceted. First, as Nawal El Saadawi has written, "We are one world (not three). . . ."[42] Strict adherence to national boundaries in literary and cultural studies can contribute to the false notion of national insularity. Furthermore, such boundaries can also justify the neglect of other English literatures by students of American or British literature. Scholars of American and British literature should be encouraged to make connections with English literature from other parts of the globe rather than abide by the limitations created by national boundaries.

In advancing such global studies of literature and culture, contextual differences cannot be ignored. It is important to avoid creating false categories, such as "postcolonial" (a designation that covers vast and vastly different parts of the world), or constructions of "women" that fail to consider other factors besides gender. Arun Mukherjee has argued that postcolonial discourse ignores differences between communities, eliminates "race" as an analytical category, and continues the colonial relationship by defining the postcolonies in terms of Western literary and cultural discourses.[43] Following Mukherjee's critique, Carole Boyce Davies concludes,

> The result of the construction of post-coloniality . . . is a replaying of the tendency in the Euro-American/modelled academy to create another sweeping, totalizing and reductive discourse to cover huge and sometimes unrelated discursive fields.[44]

Julia Watson and Sidonie Smith have presented a similar criticism of discourses that universalize the concept of "woman." "Just as there are various colonialisms or systems of domination operative historically," they write, "there are various patriarchies operative historically, not one universal 'patriarchy.' "[45]

At the same time, however, a consideration of non-Western literature can help to prevent generalizations from Western perspectives and experiences. Scholars who study traditionally marginalized literature can no longer ignorantly enforce Western cultural hegemony through their critical work. With these considerations in mind, I have included discussions of Frame and Head to avoid generalizations from American women's madness narratives. By including these works, I do not intend to universalize either the experience of madness or the elements of madness narratives; instead, my analysis not only transgresses the traditional limits of American studies but also crosses the established boundaries of area studies.

In my survey of American women's madness narratives of the nineteenth and twentieth centuries, I follow David Mora's periodization of psychiatric history.[46] Mora divides the history of psychiatry into three periods: the first half of the nineteenth century, the last half of the nineteenth century, and the first half of the twentieth century. This schema corresponds roughly to the era of so-called moral treatment, the rise of the asylum and the subsequent waning of moral treatment, and the advent of Freudian psychology and other new treatments for mental illness. The first two periods are covered together in chapter 2, and the third in chapter 3. I have added a fourth period, which is discussed in chapter 4, to correspond to the final decades of the twentieth century. This fourth period is characterized primarily by deinstitutionalization and large-scale dismantling of the mental health system, but it is also the era of "advances" in psychotropic medication and radical movements on a number of fronts, including psychiatry. Each chapter briefly considers developments in psychiatric treatment and relevant cultural factors in addition to analyzing the narratives of the period.

Through an examination of women's madness narratives, the present study traces the history of psychiatric treatment in the United States from the decades immediately following the Civil War to the present day. In so doing, this study demonstrates a general pattern in women's autobiographical accounts of psychiatric treatment. While nineteenth-century autobiographies tend to point out the failures of society in the treatment of the insane, twentieth-century narratives are more likely to emphasize psychopathology and extol the virtues of psychiatric treatment. In the late twentieth century, however, several important women's madness narratives neither advocate institutional reform nor passively accept individual pathology. These works are often revolutionary in form as well as content, and, as a result, have greater artistic and political import.

Many of the narratives that I consider have been largely ignored by scholars, although I also discuss well-known writers, such as Charlotte Perkins Gilman and Kate Millett. My selection of texts reflects my desire to find significant madness narratives rather than to analyze the psychiatric history of famous women writers. Substantial scholarly work has already been done in the latter area, particularly in regard to Sylvia Plath. In addition, numerous studies exist on madness in literature, and I try to avoid duplicating previous scholarship on cultural representations of madness.[47] Instead, I focus on largely neglected works that deserve more scholarly attention.

Chapter 2 focuses on nineteenth-century autobiographies and their relationship to social reform movements, including the "first wave" of feminism in the United States. After summarizing the beginnings of modern psychiatry, from the work of Philippe Pinel and William Tuke to the rise of the asylum, I discuss madness narratives by Elizabeth Packard, Ada Metcalf, Lydia Smith, Clarissa Lathrop, Anna Agnew, and Margaret Starr. Except for Packard's autobiographies, these works are relatively unknown. Together they provide an important account of the treatment of women mental patients and illustrate the legal vulnerability of women during the late nineteenth century. My analysis shows that, during the nineteenth century, women used life writing as a way of rebelling against the medical establishment and advocating for asylum reform.

In chapter 3, I use the concept of internalized oppression to account for the acceptance of psychiatric diagnoses by women in the twentieth century. Through an analysis of narratives by Jane Hillyer, Lucy Freeman, and Barbara Field Benziger, I illustrate how the women of this era tended to "testify against themselves" by seeing mental illness as a "prison" and psychiatrists as potential liberators. Because of the authors' apparent desire to avoid social stigmatization by presenting their stories as fiction, I discuss works that are not strictly autobiographies. Beginning with this chapter, I consider autobiographical novels, such as Joanne Greenberg's *I Never Promised You a Rose Garden*, and other narratives that fall outside a strict definition of autobiography.

Chapters 4 and 5 describe the movement away from both advocacy for institutional reform and passive acceptance of individual psychopathology. These chapters explore the revolutionary aspects of contemporary madness narratives by focusing on works by Mary Jane Ward, Susanna Kaysen, Jill Johnston, Kate Millett, Janet Frame, and Bessie Head. Chapter 4 discusses how Ward's *The Snake Pit* and recent madness narratives, especially Millett's *The Loony-Bin Trip*, challenge psychiatric practice and even the very notion of mental illness. In the course of describing her own experiences of "mental illness" and forced hospitalization, Millett advocates new ways of thinking about the mind and its capabilities.

Chapter 5 traces the union of aesthetics and politics in the madness narratives of Janet Frame and Bessie Head. The chapter begins by analyzing Frame's *Faces in the Water* and her autobiographies.[48] The analysis includes a discussion of Frame's struggle to claim her vocation as a writer in the face of cultural imperialism, economic impoverishment, and personal trauma. Frame's account of her "madness" illustrates the influence of patients' socioeconomic class on their treatment. Her psychiatric diagnosis, "schizophrenia," defines her experiences, and her narratives raise questions about the nature of creativity and the vocation of the artist.

The last part of chapter 5 discusses Head's madness narratives, particularly her autobiographical novel, *A Question of Power*.[49] In this section I argue that *A Question of Power* represents a creative synthesis of personal, political, and even cosmic struggle, as she addresses questions of power and evil in the context of contemporary Africa (i.e., South Africa and Botswana). In *A Question of Power*, the evils of racism and colonialism are intertwined with the experience of madness. Head's questions of power are played out in a metaphysical drama between good and evil that reflects the injustice of apartheid South Africa.

The study concludes with a discussion of the relevance of madness narratives to contemporary debates about the care of the so-called mentally ill in the United States. An analysis of women's madness narratives invites us to interrogate the questions of power that not only motivated the women to write but also shaped their stories. Ultimately, this study asks its readers to listen to "mad" women and allow their narratives to have an important place in the development of social policy and the transformation of cultural attitudes involving "mental illness" and its treatment.

2

Writing as Rebellion: Elizabeth Packard, Ada Metcalf, Lydia Smith, Clarissa Lathrop, Anna Agnew, and Margaret Starr

IN THE LATTER HALF OF THE NINETEENTH CENTURY, ELIZABETH Packard, Ada Metcalf, Lydia Smith, Clarissa Lathrop, and Anna Agnew, all of whom had been incarcerated in asylums for the insane, published autobiographies of their experiences. Packard, Metcalf, Smith, and Lathrop were committed involuntarily and wrote their accounts in part to expose the problems of forced hospitalization and the treatment of mental patients. Although Agnew sought medical attention for her distress, the conditions she endured while confined in the state asylum at Indianapolis moved her to protest the treatment of women inmates.

Although modern treatment of the insane represented significant improvements in comparison with the cruelties of the prescientific age, the latter part of the nineteenth century was a prime time to advocate for changes in the care of mental patients. Many of the grosser brutalities of the premodern era had been eradicated, but abusive treatment had not disappeared altogether. In the early nineteenth century, hospitals were relatively small and practiced "moral treatment." As hospitals housed greater numbers of patients, standards of care declined significantly from earlier in the century.

Moral treatment, which is traditionally seen as the first humanitarian approach to the treatment of the insane, was introduced by William Tuke (in England) and Philippe Pinel (in France). Historians of psychiatric practice with a positive view of moral treatment generally define it as "compassionate and understanding treatment of innocent sufferers."[1] According to J. Sanbourne Bockoven, "Moral treatment is of great significance in the history of psychiatry," because "It was the first practical effort made to provide systematic and responsible care for an appreciable number of the mentally ill, and it was eminently successful in achieving recoveries."[2] The success of moral treatment convinced many physicians of Pinel's thesis that, in most cases, the etiology of mental illness was not organic.[3]

The asylum environment was seen as an extremely important aspect of the care of mental patients during the era of moral treatment. Tuke modeled his "Retreat" on Quaker communities, which were separated from the rest of society. The internal operation of the Retreat was structured like a family, with Tuke as the paterfamilias. The inmates were expected to conform to the expectations of the asylum environment, which reinforced the "moral" values of industry (i.e., individual labor), obedience, and conformity. As a result, the mad were conceptualized as morally flawed rather than medically ill. As Michel Foucault writes,

> the madman, as a human being originally endowed with reason, is no longer guilty of being mad; but the madman, as a madman, and in the interior of that disease of which he is no longer guilty, must feel morally responsible for everything within him that may disturb morality and society, and must hold no one but himself responsible for the punishment he receives.[4]

In *Madness and Civilization*, Foucault problematizes the saintly images of Tuke and Pinel as liberators of the insane and asserts that their work must be reevaluated. According to Foucault, "Tuke created an asylum where he substituted for the free terror of madness the stifling anguish of responsibility; fear no longer raged under the seals of conscience."[5]

The key to understanding Foucault's argument lies in the meaning of "moral treatment." The phrase is somewhat misleading, and Denise Russell's term, "moral management,"[6] is less ambiguous and probably more appropriate. Moral treatment implied that the "insane" were being treated "morally" or humanely by "sane" people. However, rather than referring to the "moral" and hence compassionate care supposedly provided by the overseers of the asylum, moral treatment reflects the aim of the asylum to instill a new consciousness in each in-

mate. The inability of the insane to conform to social expectations is viewed as a moral failing in need of "treatment." At
Tuke's Retreat,

> the partial suppression of physical constraint was part of a system
> whose essential element was the constitution of a "self-restraint"
> in which the patient's freedom, engaged by work and the observa-
> tion of others, was ceaselessly threatened by the recognition of
> guilt.[7]

As Russell writes, "The patients at the Retreat were not kept
in chains and on the surface were given liberty, but in fact a
widespread system of constraints was in operation."[8]

Foucault also questions the saintly image of Pinel freeing the
mad from their chains. Although lacking the overt religious
component of Tuke's Retreat, Pinel's asylum became "a religious domain without religion, a domain of pure morality, of
ethical uniformity."[9] "Moral" treatment induces morality; as
Pinel maintained,

> I can generally testify to the pure virtues and severe principles
> often manifested by the cure. Nowhere except in novels have I seen
> spouses more worthy of being cherished, parents more tender, lov-
> ers more passionate, or persons more attached to their duties than
> the majority of the insane fortunately brought to the period of con-
> valescence.[10]

According to Foucault, Tuke and Pinel created an arbiter and
enforcer of a uniform morality in the personage of the keeper.
Through surveillance and judgment, the asylum "denounces
everything that opposes the essential virtues of society."[11]

The asylum superintendent, as paterfamilias, became the arbiter and enforcer of societal norms. Those who did not conform to societal expectations were mad, and their failing was
seen as a moral one. Russell points out that Pinel did not dispense with the use of physical restraints. According to Russell,

> Pinel stated that "one of the fundamental principles of the conduct
> one must adopt toward the insane is an intelligent mixture of affa-
> bility and firmness. When they are obstinate one must sound to-
> tally superior and unshakable so as to convince them to bow to the
> will of the directors." It may be necessary to use a "thundering

voice" and threaten with the harshest measures. "One of the major principles of the psychologic management of the insane is to break their will in a skillfully timed manner without causing wounds or imposing hard labor."[12]

Influenced by the apparent success of Tuke and Pinel, mental institutions were constructed in the United States. Supporters of asylum development not only sought to improve the living conditions of the insane poor; they were also optimistic about the possibility of curing large numbers of inmates through moral treatment. As in England and France, the organization of asylum life was the key to moral treatment. As David Rothman writes, "a precise schedule and regular work" were seen as crucial to the treatment of insanity.[13] Similarly, Ellen Dwyer maintains that fixed schedules were thought to serve a therapeutic function and that doctors "were reluctant to loosen their control of even the most trivial aspects" of their patients' lives.[14] According to Rothman, precision, certainty, regularity, and order became the "main weapons in the battle against insanity."[15] Rothman illustrates this emphasis on organization by quoting a New York physician, James Macdonald:

> the hours for rising, dressing and washing . . . for meals, labor, occupation, amusement, walking, riding, etc., should be regulated by the *most perfect precision*. . . . The utmost *neatness* must be observed in the dormitories; the meals must be *orderly* and comfortably served. . . . The physician and assistants must make their visits at *certain* hours.[16]

Work was central to the regimen of the asylum, and those who refused to work were punished. The emphasis on work reflects Calvinist and capitalist values, and the image of the asylum as a well-ordered institution mirrors the automation of American society during the industrial revolution. The forced labor of inmates, although considered therapeutic, was certainly exploitative. Restraints were not used as a matter of course, but they were among the punishments for failing to adhere to the dictates of the asylum. Like the new businesses of the industrial revolution, the institution itself seemed to take on greater importance than the individuals who were confined there. Nothing was to interfere with the hospital's precise schedule, and superintendents used every means available to them to force the inmates to conform.

While Tuke and Pinel were reforming the institutional care of the insane in Great Britain and France, Benjamin Rush, the "father" of American psychiatry, was establishing psychiatry as a medical specialty in the United States.[17] Treatment of mental patients in the United States largely followed the institutional philosophy of Tuke and Pinel, yet Rush's insistence on the physical basis of mental illness led the way for the resurgence of organic theories of insanity. Like Pinel, "Rush believed that to cure madness, the physician had to gain complete control over the person of the madman."[18] However, Rush maintained that there was a physical basis for mental illness and other social problems, such as alcoholism and criminal behavior. According to Szasz, Rush's medical conceptualization of "social problems—or of personal conduct of which he disapproved—served to justify their medical control."[19] Szasz calls this approach "medignosis," which he defines as "the doctrine that all human problems are medical diseases curable by appropriate therapeutic interventions, imposed on the patient by force if necessary."[20] In neutral terms, the theory of an underlying disease as the cause for deviant behavior is known as the medical model of mental illness.

By the middle of the nineteenth century, the philosophy of moral treatment had begun to give way to the medical model; however, continuity exists between moral treatment and disease models. "As the nineteenth century progressed," writes Russell, "medical discourse attempted to turn many moral categories into medical ones."[21] Moral treatment never eclipsed medical procedures, and somatic and behavioral inventions were often practiced in tandem. However, organic theories of mental illness exerted greater influence as the initial optimism about curing insanity waned and greater numbers of inmates were being confined to asylums. Changing attitudes about the curability of insanity seemed to reinforce the place of the asylum in modern America. In an 1877 article on the curability of insanity, Pliny Earle writes, "institutions for the *custody* and cure of the insane have become a public necessity."[22] The conclusion to the article asserts the value of asylums despite evidence of lower cure rates. Although he shows that insanity is less curable than had been believed, Earle asserts that he makes no argument against the "utility" or "practical value" of institutions for the insane. The understanding of insanity as a disease helped to justify the custodial care of apparently incurable patients. Larger state hospitals were built, and the number of patients made it difficult to practice moral treatment.

The construction of large asylums occurred partly as a result of the efforts of Dorothea Dix to eliminate abusive treatment. In the mid nineteenth century, Dix visited numerous asylums and other places of confinement. Elizabeth Packard claims to have spoken with Dix at the Illinois Asylum at Jacksonville, where Packard was incarcerated. "I regard Miss Dix as a Christian," writes Packard, "although honestly and conscientiously wrong, in sustaining our present system of Insane Asylums."[23] The level of abuse Dix observed, particularly during the 1840s, caused her to advocate for better care of the insane:

> I have myself seen *more than nine thousand idiots, epileptics, and insane, in these United States, destitute of appropriate care and protection*; and of this vast and most miserable company, sought out in *jails*, in *poorhouses*, and in *private dwellings*, there have been hundreds, nay, rather thousands, bound with galling chains, bowed beneath fetters and heavy iron balls, attached to drag-chains, lacerated with ropes, scourged with rods, and terrified beneath storms of profane execrations and cruel blows; now subject to gibes, and scorn, and torturing tricks—now abandoned to the most loathsome necessities, or subject to the vilest and most outrageous violation.[24]

Dix strongly believed that the abuses she observed could be eliminated if all the "insane poor" were housed in asylums. In 1848, she asked the U.S. Congress to allocate 5 million acres of public land for the construction of new facilities.

Dix was excited about the plan for the Utica State Hospital, which would be able to house hundreds of patients. Others were not convinced that larger hospitals were the answer. As David Gollaher writes,

> McLean's Luther Bell privately assured Dix that Utica was bound to be "the *largest* and *worst* hospital of the world." To design a monster institution for one thousand patients on the premise that its deranged inhabitants could be made to "function in military

fashion" was, he said foolishly optimistic. It was bound to become more like a prison than a hospital.[25]

Bell and others realized that the construction of large institutions would undermine the precision needed for successful moral treatment. The number of patients would also make it impossible for the asylum to function as a family. According to Gollaher, Bell believed that "Proper moral treatment called for individual attention and thus required a setting that encouraged familiarity. That had always been his goal at McLean: to live inside the institution as a paterfamilias."[26] The size of the institution interfered with the superintendent's role as observer and judge, and necessitated the employment of untrained psychiatric aides.

Despite her intentions, Dix's reform efforts contributed to the demise of moral treatment and led to the "warehousing" of large numbers of patients. Some institutions housed more than twice their capacity of patients. In 1875 John Bucknill visited an asylum in Philadelphia and described the overcrowding as "frightful." Although constructed to house 500 inmates, the asylum had 1,130 patients at the time of Bucknill's visit. "I was informed that at night beds were strewn on the floor in the corridors and on every available space of flooring," writes Bucknill, "so that there was no place without beds, some upon bedsteads and some upon the floors."[27] In addition to the crowded conditions, Bucknill laments the patients' lack of occupation and the frequent use of restraints—indications of the demise of moral treatment. As physicians increasingly viewed mental illness as an organic condition and larger institutions were constructed to house greater numbers of patients, moral treatment gave way to custodial care. Expenditures were reduced, the ratio of patients to physicians increased, and much of the care was relegated to untrained and poorly paid attendants. At Utica, for example, four assistant physicians were responsible for the care of 690 patients.[28] The accounts of Packard, Metcalf, Smith, Lathrop, and Agnew indicate that doctors had little contact with patients and that patients were frequently mistreated by asylum attendants.

In addition to being abused and neglected, mental patients were denied certain "basic rights," particularly the ability to communicate with the outside world. Although inhumane from a contemporary vantage point, in the nineteenth century the restriction of a mental patient's basic rights was understood to be therapeutic. Even large asylums retained the ability to isolate and control, and justified their actions as therapeutic. Family members were discouraged from coming to the asylum, lest they interfere with the patient's recovery. Correspondence between patients and their family members was also discouraged, and, as the women's narratives show, patients were typically denied writing materials. Commitment laws facilitated speedy incarceration by family members without judicial proceedings,[29] which is evidenced particularly by the accounts of Packard, Smith, and Lathrop.

Although efforts were made to isolate the patient from the outside world, the outside world could not be completely shut out from the asylum. In particular, superintendents realized that isolation would breed mistrust, and "citizens had to be assured that cruel practices would be prohibited."[30] At Utica, for instance, twenty-seven hundred visitors toured the grounds in a typical year.[31] According to Rothman, the public was encouraged to tour the asylum, but contact between patients and their family members was limited as much as possible.

Packard, Metcalf, Smith, Lathrop, and Agnew were among those who advocated for greater rights for mental patients, particularly incarcerated women. Their autobiographies were also contemporaneous with the growing movement for women's rights. In general, the late nineteenth century was a time of advocacy for a number of social and humanitarian causes. Many of the reforms called for by women mental patients were directly connected to the lack of women's rights. Packard and Smith were committed by their husbands, and their social status as women enabled their incarceration. Estelle Jelinek writes that mental institutions were often used to confine outspoken women, and she considers the accounts of defiance by incarcerated women to be among the first expressions of feminism in American literature.[32]

Elizabeth Packard's strong support of equal rights for women was undoubtedly reinforced by her commitment to the Illinois Asylum at Jacksonville. Packard was incarcerated from 1861 to 1863, an experience she describes as "be[ing] entombed three years in a living cemetery."[33] Her autobiography was published numerous times under various titles, beginning with *The Prisoner's Hidden Life; or, Insane Asylums Unveiled* in 1867. Packard was committed by her husband, a Presbyterian minister, after she persisted in expressing—and teaching—views that contradicted the doctrines of the church. Packard rejected the doctrine of total depravity as illogical and unbiblical. Describing her commitment, she writes, "the only offense my persecutors claim I have committed, is, that I have dared to be true to these my honest convictions, and to give utterance to these views in a Bible-class."[34] Her classes grew, and if Packard had not been removed, the congregation might have split over the issue of total depravity.

It is not surprising that she conceived of her incarceration as persecution and compared her commitment to the Inquisition. For Packard, insanity had replaced heresy as a label of social control:

> Had I lived in the sixteenth instead of the nineteenth century my husband would have used the laws of the day to punish me as a heretic. . . . In other words, instead of calling me by the obsolete title of heretic, he modernizes his phrase by substituting insanity instead of heresy as the crime for which I am now sentenced to endless imprisonment in one of our Modern Inquisitions.[35]

Although she does not doubt that insanity exists, Packard states that many people—particularly women—were being falsely incarcerated in asylums. According to Packard, "Much that is now called insanity will be looked upon by future ages with a feeling similar to what we feel toward those who suffered as witches in Salem, Massachusetts."[36]

Women were particularly vulnerable to psychiatric imprisonment. At the time that Packard was incarcerated, Illinois law gave men the authority to commit their wives involuntarily to psychiatric hospitals; the only stipulation was that the patient needed to be admitted by the hospital superintendent. With the assistance of Dr. Andrew McFarland, Packard's husband committed her to the Illinois State Hospital at Jacksonville. As a married woman, she had no legal recourse:

> I found that my personal liberty, and personal identity, were entirely at the mercy of Mr. Packard and Dr. McFarland; that no law of the Institution or of the State, recognized my identity while a

married woman; therefore, no protection, not even the criminal's right of self-defence, could be extended to me.[37]

Packard used every means at her disposal to resist incarceration. She refused to walk to the train to Jacksonville and had to be dragged to the station. Once admitted to the asylum, she was at first cordial to McFarland—perhaps hoping he would release her—but eventually she wrote him a letter of censure that resulted in her transfer to a ward for more disturbed patients.

When Packard was finally released by the Board of Trustees of the Jacksonville Asylum, she was once again utterly subject to the authority of her husband. She learned that he planned to commit her to Northampton Asylum in Massachusetts and obtained a writ of habeas corpus so that she could not be committed without a hearing. Szasz notes that this must have been "one of the earliest writs of habeas corpus sustained by a mental patient in the United States."[38] The hearing upheld Packard's sanity and allowed her to escape her husband's control.

As a result of her experiences, Packard learned firsthand of the legal vulnerability of women. In addition, she gained an understanding of the mistreatment of psychiatric patients. She placed the burden of responsibility on the government. She believed that the "fundamental principle of God's Government" is "an equality of rights to all accountable moral agents" and that "Our government can never echo this heavenly principle, until it defends 'equal rights,' independent of sex or color."[39] She insisted that the government, "whose chief intent and purpose is, to protect the weak against the usurpation of the strong, should not allow the husband to rule over the wife in any other sense than that of protection."[40] She makes a similar point about "despotic" superintendents. "While the Superintendents are guilty in abusing their power," she writes, "I say that Government which sustains oppression by its laws, is the first transgressor."[41] She maintains that "absolute unlimited power always tends towards despotism—or an usurpation and abuse of others' rights."[42]

One of the abuses that Packard describes is the isolation of the patients, who were cut off from the outside world. During Packard's hospitalization, patients were not allowed to have writing materials. Yet, despite the prohibition of writing materials, Packard recorded the abuses she witnessed and her own experiences. She hid her writing in the backing of a mirror that she had brought from home. "I did this," she writes,

> thinking that if I should be killed there, it might some time be found, and tell the cause of my sudden or mysterious death; or if ever I should be liberated, it might be a vindication of my sanity, and explain the reason for my being retained so long.[43]

The mirror constitutes a significant symbol for resistance through autobiographical writing. As Wood points out, Packard's mirror "comes to represent her maintenance of a sense of sanity and selfhood."[44] The diary allows Packard to record her experiences and provides a touchstone for her own sense of reality. "[T]his mirror, like myself, seemed destined to elude all attacks upon its destruction," she writes. "The document within it, and the spirit within me, seemed alike invulnerable!"[45] Her journal became a mirror of asylum life and helped sustain her sense of self.

Packard's understanding of her situation was highly influenced by her religious beliefs. She looked for God's providence in her incarceration and decided that she was placed in the institution for a reason. She believed that her purpose was to ease the suffering of other patients. During her incarceration, she attempted to protect the inmates from beatings and other abusive treatment. After her release, she successfully worked for reforms. Packard was largely responsible for changes in the commitment laws and for the establishment of basic rights for mental patients, particularly the right to correspond with the outside world.[46] She fought for personal liberty bills that would enforce the patient's right to a jury trial. Her efforts brought national attention to commitment practices and helped promote legislation to prevent the incarceration of sane individuals and to protect the rights of married women.

Although Packard's activities can be seen as part of a national movement for asylum reform, the Association of Medical Superintendents of American Institutions for the Insane portrayed her as a solitary and insane crusader. She was referred to as a "handsome and talkative crazy woman" in the association's publication, the *American Journal of Insanity*, and her actions were seen as a personal attack against McFarland for

failing to return her affections.[47] McFarland summarized
Packard's case during the annual meeting of the association in
1863.[48] Although McFarland did not name Packard, she was
later identified as McFarland's anonymous patient by John
Gray, the superintendent of the Utica asylum and editor of the
American Journal of Insanity.[49] Despite numerous attempts to
discredit her, Packard was able to sway public opinion, and
her autobiographical writing played an important role in her
work for asylum reform.

Modern Persecution, which includes an account of Packard's
reform efforts as well as writings by other incarcerated
women, remains the best-known woman's madness narrative
of the nineteenth century. The success of Packard's narrative
probably encouraged other women to tell their stories. Packard was admired by reformers and sympathizers across the
country; Ada Metcalf even dedicated her narrative, *Lunatic
Asylums, and How I Became an Inmate of One*, to Packard. The
dedication reads, "To my friend, Mrs. E.P.W. Packard, who has
nobly sacrificed much, in behalf of that most unfortunate class
of humanity, the 'insane.' " She also calls Packard "earth's no-
blest champion of the oppressed."[50]

Metcalf was a patient at the Southern Ohio Lunatic Asylum
in 1869 and 1873; she claims that she was suffering from physical ailments and was never insane. Her doctor persuaded her
to go to the asylum in 1869; Metcalf, unaware of the conditions
at the asylum, did not question the doctor's advice. She spent
five months at the asylum, and, when she left, she was convinced that she had been "humbugged."[51] Claiming to have
been misled about the care she would receive at the asylum,
she writes, "there must be a vast deal of 'humbuggery' in connection with asylums that is hidden from the public by various
disguises."[52] The purpose of her narrative, therefore, is to en-
lighten the public about the true nature of asylums, and she
"take[s] up [her] pen to strike against *the deadening effects of
Insane Asylums* in their present condition."[53]

Some of Metcalf's complaints stem from being incarcerated
with "lunatics"—and having to eat and sleep with them—but
she does not spend much of her book asserting her sanity. Instead, she focuses on the difference between public perceptions
of asylums and the realities of the conditions there. She refers
to state institutions for the insane as "Unqualified Curses,"

"Inquisitorial Prisons," "Detestable Hell-holes," "Slaughter Houses," "Whited Sepulchres," and "Plague Spots on Our National Escutcheon."[54] She calls attendants liars and "*non*-attendants,"[55] but she reserves her strongest language for physicians. Metcalf describes Doctor Heutis, who committed her on both occasions, as "cracked-brained" and "partially insane," and refers to a young superintendent as "the Great Boy Superintendent."[56] Writing of doctors in general, she says:

> the doctor—the individual who has succeeded fairly or unfairly, as the case may be, in getting an M.D. attached to his name, though but a stupid, witless donkey,—if he asserts anything, in some communities, the profoundest sage may reason in vain to confute it.[57]

Like Packard, she compares psychiatric incarceration with trials for witchcraft:

> The doctors asserted the existence of witches; and the people, with frenzied excitement, soon hunted and dragged forth the weak and defenceless, the law arraigned, tried, and convicted them; then pronounced the death penalty, and enforced it. And presumptuous ignorance never opened its eyes to look into this indiscriminate rashness, until its folly began to involve the more honored.[58]

Making a parallel between witch hunts and psychiatric commitment, Metcalf writes, "The witches are still hung; and the people, unknowingly, are aiding and abetting the deed!"[59]

Metcalf also echoes Packard in her condemnation of the system of "one-man power."[60] Metcalf blames false commitment on the absolute power of the superintendent and strongly objects to the unquestioned authority granted to physicians:

> Now the law of admittance of persons into asylums, as it stands on the statute books of Ohio to-day, grants liberty to any physician who may be termed "respectable,"—and one may pass for "respectable" and yet be knave or fool—to file an affidavit in the office of the Probate judge . . . to the effect that a certain individual is insane. And by this act that person can be deprived of his or her personal liberty![61]

Although the commitment laws maintained the one-man power system, the power of the doctor encompassed more than commitment. As Metcalf writes, "Doctor Heutis had me stamped with lunacy, and in his power. He had usurped control over both my body and soul."[62] When she is admitted, the asylum doctor directs his questions to Dr. Heutis. Although Metcalf is present, Dr. Heutis is asked such questions as "Where was she born?" and "How old is she?" Metcalf does not correct him when he provides inaccurate information; Heutis's power prevents her from contradicting him.

According to Metcalf, the injustice that results from the system of one-man power would be prevented if a jury trial were required before an individual could be committed to an institution. In her own case, she was forced to return to the Southern Ohio Lunatic Asylum in 1873. "I did not intend to go," she writes, "and did not for one moment think that such a preposterous thing would be done as that of forcing me into an Asylum."[63] Because she knew of the conditions at the asylum, she objected to going there; however, she was unable to escape incarceration. As Metcalf writes,

> I had no recourse to save myself. . . . I was ignorantly and unjustly dragged from my house a lunatic—made subservient to the will of others, and placed in confinement, as if I were incapable of rational discernment, or had been guilty of some offence, or crime.[64]

With the aid of her brother, Metcalf left the asylum after four months; she later avoided a subsequent commitment by making it known that she would obtain a writ of habeas corpus and, therefore, would have to be granted a hearing.

Metcalf focuses on unjust commitment procedures, but she also exposes the mistreatment of asylum inmates. She describes suicide attempts and deaths from negligence at the asylum, and points out that asylums often incite rather than prevent suicide. Metcalf appears to consider "imprisonment within a lunatic asylum" to be a fate "worse than death" for anyone—sane or insane.[65] She writes,

> there are some insane persons placed in those institutions, who become sane while there, and leave them; but it is not, in my opinion, owing to any benefit they derived by being an inmate of one of the "Hell-holes"—called asylums for the insane, by those ignorant of them.[66]

Metcalf calls for greater scrutiny of asylums and appeals to citizens to make themselves aware of the true conditions at psychiatric institutions. "It is time the gaping world that stalks through asylum halls, and the stupid world at home, knew something of the real life within those stately structures," she writes.[67] Although one of her main purposes in writing *Lunatic Asylums* was to inform the public, she also challenges her readers. As long as the victims of these asylums are "meanly imposed upon," she writes, "the people outside unconsciously are sharers in these impositions."[68] Metcalf's narrative stands out because it confronts readers with their responsibility for psychiatric justice.

Lydia Smith and Clarissa Lathrop, whose narratives were published in 1879 and 1890, respectively, also claimed that they were unjustifiably incarcerated. Like Elizabeth Packard, Smith was incarcerated by her husband. According to Smith, her husband committed her because he was interested in another woman. She was first taken to an asylum in Canandaigua, New York; from there she was escorted to the Michigan Asylum for the Insane at Kalamazoo by her husband's brother, who pretended to be taking her home. Unlike Packard, who was released by the Board of Trustees of the Jacksonville Asylum, Smith escaped from the Kalamazoo Asylum. After her escape, she initiated a process to prove her sanity:

> Immediately after my safe arrival among friends I wrote to Judge Dickenson, of Hillsdale, informing him of my escape from the asylum, and demanding an investigation, telling him I would appoint two physicians, and he could appoint two or more as he desired, and we would have it settled about my sanity or insanity.[69]

According to Smith, the investigation was successful. She writes, "The judge needed no further proof of my sanity, and in due course of time I sued for and obtained a bill of divorce."[70] She later remarried and used the surname of her second husband when she published her narrative.

Smith's autobiography serves to establish her sanity and to bring attention to abusive treatment at state asylums. In the preface to *Behind the Scenes*, Smith writes, "The design of this work is to awaken an interest in the public mind in behalf of the insane"; she also wanted to make the public aware that there are sane people "who are kept confined in an asylum either from a false belief in regard to their condition on the part of their friends, or from a desire on their part to keep them thus confined."[71] Indeed, Smith emphasizes in her autobiography that she was never insane. By offering her own experiences as a testimony, Smith "elicits the interest of the public, and invites and DEMANDS an investigation."[72]

Behind the Scenes does what its title promises: it describes the conditions in asylums—according to Smith's perception. Her description of the admission process shows how patients were stripped of their former identity and dehumanized as mental patients. "On the patient's arrival at the asylum they were first put into a bath," writes Smith. She believes the bath to be "necessary and perfectly right, if done in a proper way." She mainly objects to the "inhuman manner" in which she was "plunged" into the bath.[73] Yet, the admission bath can be viewed symbolically as a rite of passage into the asylum, in which the inmate becomes a nonentity. According to Smith, attendants intentionally try "to break the will and make [the patients] obedient." She writes,

> They commence a course of treatment at first to keep them in subjection, and for fear they may need it. The attendants are afraid the patients may sometime get the upper hand of them, and, to intimidate and make them submissive, use these hard and cruel modes of punishment as soon as the patient is brought to the asylum.[74]

After the admissions bath, Smith is subjected to forms of various mechanical restraints, including the protection-bed, which was commonly referred to as the "crib" because of its construction.[75] Her hands are confined in a "muff," which secures them as firmly as the stocks, and she is confined by a leather belt. "This belt is sufficiently long to fasten at the back," she writes, "so as to let the patient walk, but closely confined; or to fasten to a seat, or bench, thus keeping the patient in a sitting position."[76] Rather than being confined to a bench, Smith is placed in a "crib." A crib, she writes,

> is a square box, on which is a cover, made to close and lock, and has huge round posts, separated so as to leave a small space between for ventilation. The strap attached to the "muff" was fastened to the "crib" in such a manner as to tighten around my waist,

and across the pit of my stomach, with such a pressure that it actually seemed to me that I could not breathe. My feet were fastened to the foot of the "crib" so tight, and remained there so long, that when they did unfasten them they were swollen so that it was impossible for me to stand upon them.[77]

While she was restrained, Smith's medicine was given to her by forcing her mouth open with a wedge. Smith describes the wedge as being "five or six inches in length, one inch thick at one end, and tapered down to an eighth of an inch in thickness."[78] According to Smith, five of her teeth were either knocked out or broken off the first time the wedge was used on her. "This was my first experience in an insane asylum," Smith comments. "I did not know where I was, and thought it must be some horrible den of iniquity."[79]

The majority of Smith's narrative is concerned with her internment at the Kalamazoo Asylum. Behind the Scenes particularly condemns Dr. E. H. VanDeusen, the superintendent of the Kalamazoo Asylum, whom Smith accuses of trying to kill her to protect himself from criminal charges. She also accuses him of gross mismanagement and violation of Michigan asylum laws. She cites laws mandating that no patient be injured, that every patient be seen as often as his or her condition requires, that two doctors concur before commitment that a person is in need of treatment (to prevent the incarceration of sane people), and that "no ignorant or unprincipled attendants" be employed.[80] "I would willingly give the remainder of my life," she writes, "if by so doing I could save one soul from suffering what I have suffered in the Kalamazoo asylum."[81]

Smith's emphasis on illegal activity in general and her focus on VanDeusen in particular probably stem from investigations of practices at the asylum that were in process at the time that Behind the Scenes was published. In 1878 Nancy Newcomer, a former patient at the hospital, sued VanDeusen for false imprisonment and assault and battery. The jury found in favor of Newcomer and awarded her six thousand dollars in damages. Although a subsequent trial reversed the original judgment, public outcry about abusive treatment at the asylum led to an investigation into conditions at the Kalamazoo Asylum. Stories were circulating that "sane people were often confined in hospitals for the insane," writes Rush McNair. "Many people looked upon every doctor as a potential body-snatcher."[82]

Smith was among the first to testify during the state hearings. A newspaper account claims that her "nerve shattering yarn was the merest moonshine" because it was contradicted by the "the testimony of reliable witnesses and the records of the institution."[83] The article states that Smith was "considered to be in a very fair condition of mental health" and explains her story by means of the theory of the "memory of delusions." Smith

> could not be said to have committed perjury. It is a curious fact connected with the restoration of a patient to sanity that some of the delusions which possess the mind while unsound are still believed in implicitly.[84]

Smith's testimony, then, was viewed as less reliable than that of others because it was assumed that she had indeed been insane while she was confined to the Kalamazoo Asylum.

Behind the Scenes serves as Smith's public testimony to the misuse of commitment laws and to the abusive treatment of patients. She presents her narrative as a testimony. Following Smith's preface is a statement signed by several references, all of whom attest that she was never insane. Then an account of her parentage is presented, apparently another proof of the author's credibility. After the table of contents, Smith presents her narrative as legal testimony. The following statement appears immediately before the first chapter of the narrative: "Lydia A. Smith, being duly sworn, deposes and says that the contents and statements contained in this book are true in substance and in fact." This statement is certified by a notary public.

By writing an autobiographical account of her incarceration, Smith is able to control the presentation of her narrative and to define the meaning of her experiences. Smith's madness narrative allows her to claim the agency denied her by public officials and the local press. *Behind the Scenes* gives Smith the opportunity to tell her own story to a wider audience and assert that she was sane both before and after her incarceration. In so doing, she exposes abusive treatment in asylums and advocates for better commitment laws and greater rights for mental patients.

Packard and Smith were committed by their husbands; Clarissa Lathrop, who never married, was committed by her mother and sister. She was incarcerated at the State Asylum at Utica, New York, from October 1880 to December 1882. The superintendent of Utica at the time was the powerful John P. Gray, who had been appointed in 1854. According to Lathrop, Gray (or Grey, to follow Lathrop's spelling) and Utica were synonymous.[85] She considered him to be "unscrupulous, and careless or indifferent to all but pecuniary advantages."[86] Gray's authority at Utica, though not unchallenged, was unshakable. As Ellen Dwyer writes, "Anyone who challenged Gray's power, even one of his handpicked assistant physicians, was quickly discharged."[87]

During his tenure at Utica, Gray faced both formal investigations and informal challenges regarding financial matters and patient care. Gray's adversaries not only included politicians and social reformers, but also neurologists.[88] In the late nineteenth century, intense debates raged between neurologists and asylum physicians over asylum practices and the very nature of psychiatry. One of the strongest advocates for asylum reform was S. Weir Mitchell, who expressed his views at the annual meeting of the American Medico-Psychological Association in 1894.[89] Even before Mitchell issued his call for reform, however, neurologists had not only objected to asylum practices but had also claimed psychiatry as a branch of their own specialty.[90] At the extreme, asylum physicians were viewed as monopolizing the study of mental pathology and practicing an unscientific—or perhaps even barbaric—form of medicine.

During the 1870s and 1880s, several investigations focused on the use of restraints at Utica, particularly the infamous Utica crib.[91] Lathrop refers to the crib as "Dr. Grey's pet instrument of torture."[92] Although she was never confined to a crib, Lathrop explains that "patients were often placed in one as a punishment, or to save the attendant the trouble of watching them, or to avoid their requests for care, etc."[93] She writes that confinement in a crib, which kept the patient in a recumbent position and allowed little movement, impeded the circulation and could result in cerebral disease. Patients had died while confined in a crib, and, in 1884, the Utica Asylum was investigated following the death of a patient. Asylum officials were declared innocent of knowingly abusing patients.[94]

Female patients suffered many other abuses besides physical

restraint. According to Lathrop, the doctors at Utica frequently raped women patients. "I believe," she writes, "that
few patients escape the wanton lust of the physicians."[95] She
claims that doctors defend themselves by asserting that a
woman patient's belief that she has been raped " 'is the most
common delusion of insane patients.' "[96] Lathrop claims to
have been drugged and raped repeatedly. "I was at the mercy
of unscrupulous and vicious men," she writes, "with no one to
appeal to for help or redress, with no escape, no refuge,—
powerless to protect myself."[97] The investigating committee of
1884 recommended that Utica employ female physicians, if
only to protect female patients from their fantasies of sexual
abuse.[98] In *A Secret Institution*, Lathrop strongly agrees that
female patients should be attended by women doctors.

Lathrop also calls for complete freedom of correspondence
for asylum inmates and greater public access to the wards. In
1889 Utica administrators had closed the wards to casual visitors and erected high wooden walls around the asylum.[99] According to Lathrop, the secrecy surrounding asylum life
increased the vulnerability of the patients, particularly women
patients. "Throw open wide your asylum doors to the public
and the medical profession," she writes, "allow free correspondence and employ women physicians on the wards, and such
terrible charges will no more be made."[100] Lathrop sees rape as
one of the factors that causes or worsens insanity among female inmates. As a result of her feelings of sexual vulnerability, she vows to do everything in her power to help the inmates
of Utica:

> It was when suffering the greatest mental agony on account of
> these terrible experiences, that I made the solemn vow, *"That if the
> Lord would spare my life to leave that horrible prison, I would de-
> vote the rest of my life, if necessary, to the cause of the insane, par-
> ticularly those of my own sex."*[101]

Deprived of writing materials and unable to mail letters to
anyone but her mother and sister, Lathrop devised ways to
send letters. On one occasion she gave a letter to a member of
the investigating committee during his visit to the asylum; she
also concealed a letter in a ball of yarn. Eventually, James Silk-
man, an asylum reformer and former inmate of Utica, learned

of Lathrop's situation and served Dr. Gray with a writ of habeas corpus. As a result, Lathrop appeared before a jury and was found to be sane. After her release from Utica, Lathrop became an advocate for mental patients, and she joined the Anti-Kidnapping League and Lunacy Reform Union.[102] "One aim, one purpose actuated all my endeavors," she writes,

> that was to help the poor victims of the Utica Asylum, and the desire to improve the social and mental condition of the insane. For this I gladly labored night and day, and every dollar I could save was consecrated to this sacred cause.[103]

Like Packard, Metcalf, and Smith, Lathrop expresses concern over the commitment of sane persons and the abusive treatment of asylum patients. Lathrop writes that the commitment laws, as regulated by the legislature in 1889, would be suitable if they were followed to the letter; however, she also says that if commitment papers were *"swept away*, there would be no necessity for an expensive State Commission of Lunacy, such as is provided for under present regulations."[104] Lathrop fears that the commissioners may act unscrupulously, particularly for monetary gain, and commit sane people to Utica. She claims that most asylum abuses could be corrected by reducing the power of asylum superintendents and governing boards. According to Lathrop, the respectability of the board members and their confidence in the asylum superintendent fosters abuse because the board protects the asylum's reputation in the community. However, "The most powerful evil," according to Lathrop, "is 'the one man power' of the asylum superintendent, whose fiat is final as to the sanity or insanity of his unfortunate patient."[105] Lathrop critiques the power invested in the superintendent and argues, like Packard and Metcalf, that no individual should have such power.

Although the accounts by Smith and Lathrop have much in common with earlier madness narratives, there are important differences. Jelinek classifies the autobiographies of Smith and Lathrop as "exposés" and links them to sensational accounts by women prisoners and ex-nuns.[106] She finds a "sensational-exotic strain" in nineteenth-century women's autobiographies as well as a concern with social reform.[107] Indeed, Smith and Lathrop rely more on sensationalism than Packard and Metcalf, who offer a more sophisticated level of analysis. Even the titles of Smith's and Lathrop's narratives, *Behind the Scenes; or, Life in an Insane Asylum* and *A Secret Institution*, reveal the influence of sensationalist literature and journalistic exposés. They emphasize the horror of being of imprisoned with maniacs and lunatics, who are represented as grotesque if not dangerous. Yet, despite the sensational aspects of their narratives, Smith and Lathrop contributed to the asylum social reform movement of the late nineteenth century.

Anna Agnew's *From under a Cloud; or, Personal Reminiscences of Insanity*, published in 1886,[108] differs from the accounts by Packard, Metcalf, Smith, and Lathrop. First of all, Agnew does not claim to have been unfairly incarcerated; instead, she relates her difficulties in getting others to recognize that she needs treatment. She never doubts that she is ill, and she attributes her recovery to the woman doctor who cared for her at the Indiana State Hospital at Indianapolis. One of her reasons for writing her autobiography is to give hope to others by showing that mental illness is not incurable. Agnew sees herself as an insane woman who was able to come out from under the "cloud" of her sickness.

As she does not view her incarceration as either unjust persecution or an unwarranted deprivation of liberty, Agnew leaves the asylum under circumstances quite different from Packard, Smith, and Lathrop. Agnew is discharged because the doctors determine that she is well; the only issue for her is to avoid being released into the control of her husband. Indeed, one of the ways that Agnew fights back against the abusive behavior of her husband—particulary his efforts to cut her off from their two children—is by writing *From under a Cloud*. She presents an unflattering portrait of her husband and describes him as a man "who deserted and tried to disgrace his wife."[109] She also makes a plea for sympathy on account of her separation from her children.

Like other nineteenth-century madness narratives, Agnew uses her autobiography to advocate for changes in the treatment of mental patients. In the introduction she objects particularly to the employment of untrained psychiatric aides. She writes,

[I] will speak freely of gross abuses, for which there is no remedy, until state laws require that none but those who are fitted for the

sacred duties of attendants upon the insane be employed—such
preparation being a complete course in a training school for
nursing.[110]

Later in the book, she reproduces a letter, which she addressed
to the Indiana legislature, regarding public access to state hospital wards. In the letter, which was also published in the *Indianapolis Herald*, Agnew writes:

> it is a duty I owe to humanity to make an appeal to the legislature
> for a law prohibiting the promiscuous visiting at [hospitals for the
> insane], and were it in my power to make you understand the posi-
> tive torture many of those peculiarly unfortunate people suffer
> from the mere presence of the throngs of impertinent morbid curi-
> osity seekers—from whom there is no escape in the wards of their
> prison—I am sure my attempt in their behalf will not be in vain.[111]

Agnew's words here are reminiscent of Packard's and Smith's.
Although Agnew does not dispute her need for treatment, she
worked to improve the conditions at state mental institutions
after her release, especially regulations allowing public access
to the wards.

As Rothman points out, asylums attempted to allay suspi-
cions by allowing the public to tour the asylum. In 1876 as
many as 11,794 citizens toured the asylum at Utica.[112] Margaret Starr, who would later be incarcerated in an asylum, recalls
visits to the asylum as a child:

> The country home of our family was on the property adjoining an
> insane asylum: a Mad-House. I visited and saw the insane fre-
> quently; their indoor entertainments, their sorrows, and afflic-
> tions, as well as their outdoor sports, were familiar to me.[113]

As Agnew's account shows, public access to the wards fulfilled
purposes other than the regulation of institutional practices.
She presents the tours of the wards as Sunday entertainment
for local residents, not unlike a freak show at a circus. Agnew
was particularly victimized, as attendants directed visitors to
the "devil's corner." As Agnew writes,

> In each ward there are generally one or more unfortunates to
> whom the attention of visitors is directed in particular, on account

of some peculiarity of "delusion". . . . of all the monstrosities in this immense "museum," I was the superlative one. Of course every body and their "uncles, and aunts, and cousins" would embrace the opportunity of seeing the devil![114]

Instead of serving to police the institution, such visits functioned more as a warning to those who would violate social codes. Prior to the advent of long-term incarceration, individuals who committed serious crimes or repeatedly broke the law were executed. These executions were understood to uphold the laws and protect the community; yet, as Rothman notes, "An execution was an ideal opportunity to alert the public to the dangers of all forms of deviant behavior."[115] According to Rothman, ministers often preached at executions, explaining the dangers of earthly sins and the fate of nonrepentant sinners in the life to come. The condemned person was encouraged to confess and convert before it was too late. When Agnew was displayed in the asylum as "the devil," visitors were simultaneously "entertained" by such a curious figure and warned to stay in line so that they do not end up in "the devil's corner." As Agnew points out, the visitor was protected by the institution:

They could have a view of the Satanic majesty at a moderately short range, when attended by a body-guard, consisting of one usher and two attendants who felt the "contempt that familiarity breeds," and as a consequence, were not afraid of the devil.[116]

Agnew's statement that the attendants were familiar with the "devil" indicates not only the contempt they had for her but also implies that their behavior revealed their familiarity with the "Satanic majesty." According to Agnew, the attendants tried to make her look demonic. "[I]n order to further mortify the little remaining self-respect, I was not compelled, as were the other patients, to change my clothing; so rags and dirt added attraction to my already miserable appearance."[117] In making Agnew "the devil," the attendants manifested their own capacity for evil.

Like Packard, Smith, and Lathrop, Agnew's incarceration made her aware of the tremendous vulnerability of women in regard to psychiatric incarceration. She writes, "from painful experience [I] consider it my duty to speak in behalf of my suffering sisters."[118] Agnew distances herself from feminists and says, "I don't think my sisters of the woman's rights party will care to claim me as one of them."[119] At the same time, however, she refers to herself as a "humble tho' aspiring sister,"[120] and many of her actions have an affinity to the growing movement for women's rights.

Agnew lived in a manner that affirmed her belief in the need for women to have greater freedom from men and from the dictates of social roles. She can be seen as a feminist despite her apparent rejection of the women's rights movement. According to Agnew, insane *women* are particularly miserable, and she calls for a greater number of women physicians. "[F]or the sake, and in behalf of suffering women—insane women in particular," she writes, "I make an appeal to the board of trustees of every female hospital for the insane in the land, for the appointment of a woman upon their medical staff."[121] Her insistence on being independent from her husband and her public advocacy on behalf of mental patients, including the publication of *From under a Cloud*, are feminist in substance if not in intention.

By publishing accounts of their experiences, Packard, Smith, Lathrop, and Agnew insist on the right to self-definition. Rather than allowing their experiences to be described in the terms advanced by the male psychiatric establishment, they claim the right to describe and interpret their own lives. Their accounts contribute to social as well as personal change by simultaneously calling for reform of mental institutions and providing a medium for the author to define her experiences for herself. In writing "for herself," each of these writers comes to some understanding of her experiences and also decides how to represent these experiences to her reading audience.

The process is not necessarily linear, however. Just as Packard's writing becomes her mirror, Metcalf, Smith, Lathrop, and Agnew also use narrative to explore as well as represent their experiences of incarceration. Their books reveal the abusive nature of commitment procedures and asylum management; at the same time, the act of writing allows the author to begin to come to terms with abuses that she herself had experienced. This type of resistance is consistent with the idea of personal healing as social change, which is asserted by twentieth-century feminist therapists and theoreticians.[122] For Packard, Metcalf, Smith, Lathrop, and Agnew, writing was a way to rebel; in their madness narratives, they reject both institutional practices and the male prerogative to define and limit the experiences of women.

Despite their success at inciting public sympathy and advocating legal changes, oppressive practices continued. Margaret Starr's 1904 narrative, *Sane or Insane? or How I Regained Liberty*, illustrates the continuation of commitment without due process and the isolation of asylum inmates from their family and friends. On the basis of the testimony of two doctors, a jury committed Starr without even meeting her. Not only was Starr ignorant of the proceedings, but the two physicians who certified her as insane never interviewed her but instead based their decision on hearsay. One of the doctors, by Starr's account, had not seen her in over two years. She was largely unacquainted with the other physician, having conversed with him on only one previous occasion—for a few minutes on a business matter. Although Starr does not offer an explanation for her unjust incarceration, there are indications that someone may have been trying to keep her from gaining control of her financial assets.

As a result of Starr's insanity hearing, of which she knew nothing until after she had escaped from the asylum, she was taken by force to an asylum. She repeatedly asks to know the reason for her detainment, "whatever has been charged against me,"[123] and when she could expect to be released. She never receives satisfactory answers to her requests. The best answer she can get is that she has been placed in the asylum for a "rest cure." Although Starr's supposed treatment differs from the "rest cure" inflicted upon many intellectually active women of the time, she is judged to have strayed from the acceptable activities of women. When she asks the head nurse why she needs the rest cure, Madam Pike replies, "Have you not written books? Is not brain work the hardest of all kinds of labor?"[124] Pike's answer betrays sexual bias in psychiatric diagnosis. Writing books is esteemed when the authors are men; however, women who write or engage in other nondomestic activities are viewed with suspicion by the medical establishment.

Starr does not discuss the double standard of psychiatric di-

agnosis. In fact, she even uses it in her favor. She reproduces
the statements of an expert witness who testified to her sanity
after her escape from the asylum. She refers to him as "the star
witness" and "a noted expert on mental diseases."[125] He testi-
fies that he found her "to be of a neurotic temperament; but
that is a trait of the American woman, especially the American
woman who is high strung, sensitive, and intelligent." He also
refers to her "mild hysteria," which he claims "is an indication
that a woman is active, energetic and ambitious, one likely to
follow ideas, or purposes to the end." When asked if mild hysteria leads to insanity, the doctor's reply is an emphatic
"never." He states that mild hysteria "has nothing to do with
insanity. Insanity is a disease of the brain. I found Miss Star
[sic] mentally far superior to the average woman. But the average American woman is hysterical."[126] In her narrative, Starr
never relates her treatment to her being a woman. She neither
accepts nor rejects medical views of women (at least not explicitly), although she also does not question her expert witness's opinions regarding American women. The injustice of
her treatment stems only from her wrongful incarceration as
insane.

However, Starr does object to the violent behavior of the
head nurse, Madam Pike, and the infringement of her legal
rights. Although Starr was able to keep a diary, she was denied
books and found it difficult to secure writing materials. "I was
denied all privileges, and admonished to be quiet," writes
Starr.

> I enquired if there were children or even grown persons whom I
> could teach the ordinary rudiments of education, or music lessons.
> I asked for the use of a dictionary, a French book, or a Latin
> book, to renew my studies in those languages; or, as I told her, any
> occupation would be acceptable.
> With the exception of three or four books from the library of the
> Institution, and five or six magazines loaned me for a few hours at
> a time, none of the above requests were ever granted to me. . . . I
> was doomed to idleness as far as Madam Pike was concerned.[127]

Repeatedly told to be quiet and barred from conversation,
Starr wrote notes to converse silently with other patients. Such
communication had to be kept secret, and Starr even sent notes

to another patient by writing on muslin and stitching the fabric into her petticoat. The two women would then exchange undergarments and remove the notes so that they could read them. Madam Pike eventually confiscated some of these notes. Pike also prevented Starr from sending letters to her friends or contacting an attorney; her friends' letters were returned to them, and they were denied the opportunity to visit Starr. Despite laws guaranteeing patients the right to send letters, Starr's letters never reached their destination. Tours of the asylum were still taking place, for Starr's friends attempted to visit her by taking advantage of public access to the wards. However, they were never permitted to visit Starr's hall.

Although Starr forms relationships with several of the patients, she considers herself sane and cruelly punished by having to associate with insane women. She worries about the stigma attached to those deemed insane, but her main objection is that she is viewed and treated as one of the insane:

> I thought over the real horrors of prison life, which have frequently been placed before the public. Take all those horrors and add what you may, the idea, the knowledge, that you are being treated as insane while in a lunatic asylum with only lunatics as associates is unparalleled for cruelty; for it dooms you to be a *nonentity!*[128]

In maintaining the distinction between sanity and insanity, Starr fails to grasp the problems of psychiatric labeling. She objects that being labeled insane makes her a "nonentity"; she does not explicitly object to the view that "insane" persons are "nonentities." Her sympathies are mainly evoked by those she deems sane and therefore unjustly incarcerated. She fails to question the institution itself, going so far as to claim that, "If you are mentally unbalanced, the Mad-House under a proper nurse, is the best place in the world for the patient, for the chances are that, through the methods used the patient will recover."[129] She compares the asylum to a school, in which incarceration functions as motivation to behave properly:

> as I noticed their efforts to improve, it looked like a class where ambition was instilled to behave with common sense, so as to regain liberty, and be sent home; as in a school where the ambition is quickened to stand at the head of the class, and win prizes.[130]

At the end of her narrative, Starr does consider the situation of those who need to be incarcerated. However, just as her main concern is for the protection of the "sane," her first appeal addresses the need for those with "afflicted minds" to have contact with people who are not "mentally sick or weak."[131] Starr encourages friends and family to make frequent visits, and decries the attempts by the institution to prohibit such contact. Although she does speak out against the lack of supervision of nursing personnel that fosters the abuse of patients and the use of restraints, particularly strait-jackets, Starr's major advocacy is for contact between inmates and the outside world. She urges relatives to visit the inmates and listen to them; she even advocates trial visits home. One of the unstated purposes for such contact is the rescue of those who no longer need to be incarcerated and confined to the company of the insane. For those who truly are insane, Starr urges family members and friends to cooperate with and participate in the treatment outlined by the institution:

> The method of curing of patients in the Asylum is for the nurse to complain to them of their particular defects. So you, their friends, assist in this method by telling the patients in plain language of their especial deficiencies, hoping thereby that the many well minds will overpower the mental defects.[132]

As the title of Starr's narrative indicates, she believes that a clear demarcation exists between sanity and insanity. She approves of incarceration and the method of treatment, and her narrative does not make the forceful appeals found in other nineteenth-century accounts. Like Packard, Metcalf, Smith, and Lathrop, Starr wants to convince her readers that she was never insane, but unlike the others, the advocacy in her narrative does not extend much beyond her own circumstances. She summarizes the proceedings of the trial that certifies her as sane and decries the laws that enabled a sane person such as herself to be committed and kept in an asylum.

Like Packard, Metcalf, Smith, Lathrop, and Agnew, Starr does not doubt that insanity exists and must be treated. However, she departs from her nineteenth-century predecessors by deemphasizing the need for better conditions in mental institutions and raising fewer questions about the treatment of asylum inmates. Although she reprints an editorial that argues that the "expert testimony" of doctors is "notoriously unreliable,"[133] Starr grants physicians a high level of expertise in diagnosing and treating the insane—provided they adequately examine the patient. By recognizing the expertise of physicians, Starr implicitly accepts the gender bias of psychiatric treatment and diagnosis. Her acceptance of the expertise of doctors to diagnose and treat "mental illness" provides an early indication of the direction taken by women's madness narratives in the twentieth century.

3

Testifying against Themselves: Charlotte Perkins Gilman, Marian King, Jane Hillyer, Joanne Greenberg, Lucy Freeman, and Barbara Field Benziger

THE TWENTIETH CENTURY WITNESSED MAJOR SHIFTS IN PSYchiatric treatment, and women's madness narratives reflect these changes. Developments in psychiatric practice, especially the theories of Sigmund Freud, continued to reinforce male dominance. At the same time, the waning of feminist activity subsequent to the passage of the Nineteenth Amendment increased women's vulnerability to misogynist psychiatric discourse. Lacking a strong alternative discourse, women accepted the interpretations of psychiatric professionals. The vast majority of twentieth-century women's madness narratives show an acceptance of psychiatric diagnoses and a reliance on the expertise of doctors. Twentieth-century madness narratives tend to be confessional in tone, and many of them were published pseudonymously or under the guise of fiction. To a certain extent, psychiatrists controlled the presentation of madness narratives by appropriating them as "case histories" or offering expert commentary. Psychiatrists exerted such influence that, even without direct involvement, they still determined the perspective of women's madness narratives. For most of the twentieth century, women internalized societal and psychiatric oppression and testified against themselves in their narratives.

Although continuities exist between the madness narratives of the nineteenth and twentieth centuries, firsthand accounts of psychiatric treatment reflect the particular characteristics of each era. Confinement, one of the dominant themes in both nineteenth-century and twentieth-century women's madness narratives, exemplifies the shift in perspective. During the nineteenth century, the limitations imposed on women by societal expectations were clearly mirrored by their experiences in mental institutions. False imprisonment is a major theme in most of the narratives of this period, and the rationale for commitment is equally important. Elizabeth Packard and Lydia Smith were committed by their husbands, and each woman's narrative indicates that she was incarcerated for her husband's convenience. Anna Agnew, who sought treatment, still fell under her husband's authority and was prevented from seeing her children. Independent women, such as Metcalf, Lathrop, and Starr, were also committed to insane asylums, and, ironically, their status as independent women might have contributed to their confinement. Without a man to protect them, other men were able to have them incarcerated. Two of these women needed help from men to gain their freedom; Metcalf was aided by her brother and Lathrop by a male reformer. Without the protection provided by a husband, women were particularly vulnerable to rape. The accounts of Smith and Lathrop indicate that doctors and other men exercised the husband's prerogative of sex on demand.

Women's experiences of incarceration mirrored the constraints placed on women in society. Outside the asylum, women were bound in corsets and other confining apparel. Inside the asylum, women were locked in their rooms or restrained in "cribs," "camisoles," and "muffs."[1] Writing of women's fashions in the 1880s, Rose Kerr states, "Costumes were conducive, not to action, but to standing. . . . The skirts, already narrowing at the knees, were still more constricting."[2] According to Elinor Roth Nugent, "The resignation of women to a role of dependency was signified by the wearing of a dress based upon a feature of dress design which made women practically helpless."[3] Women's fashions of the 1880s limited movement and distorted the natural shape of the body in ways that are analogous to mechanical restraining devices. As Nugent writes,

The silhouette of the 1880's was achieved only through the use of underclothing and corsets which molded the body into the desired contour and posture. The upper part of the body was restricted by

corsets which tilted the figure forward. The lower part of the body
was pushed backward from the waist.[4]

The tendency to name mechanical restraint devices after wom-
en's fashions supports Showalter's argument that madness is
the female malady. The common name for the protection bed,
"crib," indicates the tendency to infantilize asylum inmates, as
women were infantilized by societal constraints.

Commitment practices in the nineteenth century placed additional limitations on the lives of women. After a woman was
declared insane, she no longer had even the illusion of autonomy. Judges, lawyers, doctors, and hospital staff defined the
experiences of women mental patients, and the women's own
explanations could be seen as symptoms of insanity. Similarly,
women who were not incarcerated were often denied voice,
agency, and intellectual independence. The primary feminist
struggle at the time was the right to vote, and suffrage can be
seen as a concrete expression of voice, agency, and intellectual
independence.

During the first wave of feminism, women formed alliances
and worked together for common goals. Organizations such as
the National American Woman Suffrage Association and the
Women's Christian Temperance Union challenged the patriarchal structures of the time. Within the asylum, however, bond-
ing between women was actively discouraged—if not
thwarted—by institutional policy. Communication was difficult; Starr, for example, was repeatedly barred from convers-
ing with patients and staff members, and she and another
woman secretly communicated by stitching notes in their undergarments. Packard, Metcalf, Smith, Lathrop, and Starr
were unable to communicate with friends in the outside world.
Incarcerated women were largely unable to form the kind of
alliances that proved to be essential in winning greater rights
for women in American society.

Unlike the works discussed in the previous chapter, the madness narratives of the early to mid–twentieth century correspond to a dormant time in the struggle for women's rights.
During the period between the so-called first and second waves
of the feminist movement (from the 1920s to the 1960s), the
movement became submerged, and, for the most part, women's
madness narratives of this time period reflect the decline in

feminist discourse. Confinement remains a dominant theme in these narratives, but the image of confinement is radically reconceptualized. Instead of focusing on external oppression, such as false imprisonment, the "one-man power" of the superintendent, and the particular vulnerability of women, the writers of women's madness narratives of this era internalize their oppression and accept the expert opinions of their doctors. The diseased mind, rather than the institution, constitutes the prison, and the doctor is no longer seen as a jailkeeper but rather as an expert who has the ability to release women from the prison of mental illness.

The concept of internalized oppression provides an interpretative framework for understanding the shift in focus from societal contraints to individual psychopathology. Internalized oppression has been defined as "the incorporation and acceptance by individuals within an oppressed group of the prejudices against them within the dominant society."[5] According to Gail Pheterson,

> Internalized oppression is likely to consist of self-hatred, self-concealment, fear of violence and feelings of inferiority, resignation, isolation, powerlessness, and gratefulness for being allowed to survive. Internalized oppression is the mechanism within an oppressive system for perpetuating domination not only by external control but also by building subservience into the minds of oppressed groups.[6]

Madness narratives exemplify internalized oppression to the extent that the writers of these narratives accept the role prescribed for women in patriarchal society. According to Germaine Greer, psychiatry serves to reinforce gender roles. "As far as the woman is concerned," writes Greer, "psychiatry is an extraordinary confidence trick: the unsuspecting creature seeks aid because she feels unhappy, anxious and confused, and psychiatry persuades her to seek the cause in *herself*."[7] In women's madness narratives, internalized oppression typically involves the acceptance of the psychiatric labels and treatments prescribed by physicians and psychotherapists.

A second aspect of internalized oppression is the tendency to oppress others, particularly members of one's own group.[8] This type of horizontal violence (i.e., against other oppressed people) is also apparent in women's madness narratives. Lydia Smith and Ada Metcalf differentiated themselves from other mental patients by asserting that they themselves were not insane. Women who accepted their diagnoses resorted to other measures, many of which mirrored the oppressions of society at large. In *Reluctantly Told*, Jane Hillyer sees the hospital's failure to maintain racial and class distinctions as part of the degradation of institutionalization. Hillyer complains that she must take her meals with women of all races and social classes. Sylvia Plath's protagonist in *The Bell Jar* implicitly distinguishes herself from lesbian patients through the homophobic narrative of a relationship between a patient and a staff member.[9] These examples indicate that racism, classism, and heterosexism separated institutionalized women just as similar divisions prevented alliances between women in the movement for women's rights.

Internalized oppression can also involve the incorporation of different types of oppressive discourses. As the work of Phyllis Chesler and the research of Inge Broverman and her colleagues demonstrated, psychopathology and androcentrism are clearly related.[10] The internalized oppression of women mental patients typically reflects a multiplicity of internalized oppressions. According to Audre Lorde, "we have been taught to suspect what is deepest in ourselves, and this is the way we learn to testify against ourselves, against our feelings."[11] Once people learn to distrust their feelings, they begin to interpret their experiences in the terms perpetuated by the oppressors. As Lorde writes,

> The way you get people to testify against themselves is not to have police tactics and oppressive techniques. What you do is to build it in so people learn to distrust everything in themselves that has not been sanctioned, to reject what is most creative in themselves to begin with, so you don't even need to stamp it out.[12]

In most of the madness narratives of this era, the authors testify against themselves by viewing themselves as mentally unhealthy and accepting the limits imposed by patriarchal society. They testify against one another by imposing psychiatric labels or by expressing the sexism, racism, classism, and heterosexism of American society.

Although some elements of Agnew's *From under a Cloud* foreshadow twentieth-century madness narratives, Charlotte Perkins Gilman's autobiography, *The Living of Charlotte Perkins Gilman*, provides a bridge between the nineteenth and twentieth centuries.[13] Her story is particularly significant because she avoids internalizing her oppression and testifying against herself—even though she wrote her narrative during an era that reasserted male dominance through psychological theories. As Tomes writes,

> it was a rare woman such as Charlotte Perkins Gilman who made the connection between restrictive gender roles and women's vulnerability to emotional distress. . . . For the vast majority of nineteenth-century women, the connections between emotional distress and women's inequality, which Gilman articulated so well, appear to have remained hidden.[14]

As the following discussion will show, Gilman was also a rarity among those women who wrote madness narratives in the first part of the twentieth century.

In 1890 Gilman was treated for neurasthenia after the birth of her daughter. As Showalter points out, the majority of American neurasthenic patients were female.[15] Gilman perceived that her diagnosis was based on her sex. Although she was not institutionalized, she was given a treatment that involved confinement. Gilman consulted S. Weir Mitchell, whose famous rest cure had become the standard treatment for neurasthenia.[16] "This eminent physician," she writes, "was well versed in two kinds of nervous prostration; that of the business man exhausted from too much work, and the society woman exhausted from too much play. The kind I had was obviously beyond him."[17] Indeed, as Showalter notes, "neurasthenia was seen as an acceptable and even an impressive illness for men."[18]

Mitchell's rest cure was consistent with the prevailing opinion of the time, which conceptualized mental disease as an organic condition that could be exacerbated by environmental stress. His treatment of Gilman also reflects sex role expectations and the belief that intellectual work was harmful to women. Nervous conditions were linked with women's ambition; according to Showalter, it was believed that mental breakdown occurred "when women defied their 'nature,' attempted to compete with men instead of serving them, or sought alternatives or even additions to their maternal functions."[19] Similarly, Suzanne Poirier writes,

> Those who survived the Weir Mitchell Rest Cure were nearly as one in recognizing their emotional highs and lows as a part of their overall psychological makeup, emotions that were only magnified when these women were allowed no other focus for their attention. Because their interests lay outside the recognized sphere of a woman's world they received little support and often little sympathy from their physicians, their society, and sometimes even their own family. These women had to define themselves to themselves, often in defiance of all authority figures around them.[20]

The Weir Mitchell rest cure began with a period of complete bed rest. Showalter describes the typical regimen as follows: "For six weeks the patient was isolated from her family and friends, confined to bed, forbidden to sit up, sew, read, write, or to do any intellectual work, visited daily by the physician, and fed and massaged by a nurse."[21] Gilman relates that after a month of bed rest, Mitchell sent her home with this prescription:

> "Live as domestic a life as possible. Have your child with you all the time. . . . Lie down an hour after each meal. Have but two hours' intellectual life a day. And never touch pen, brush or pencil as long as you live."[22]

The rest cure only made Gilman's condition worse. She writes, "I went home, followed those directions rigidly for months, and came perilously near to losing my mind."[23] Because her condition was usually alleviated by being away from home, Gilman decided instead to seek a divorce. Her condition improved, but she claims in her autobiography that the rest cure had lasting deleterious effects.

Gilman's autobiography does not contain an extended critique of psychiatric treatment. She stresses the chronicity of her condition, but her experiences are primarily described in a single chapter. Her autobiography spans most of her life and does not focus on psychiatric abuses; however, other incidents in *The Living of Charlotte Perkins Gilman* express her condemnation of psychiatric treatment. In addition to criticizing psychiatric treatment in her autobiography, which was not published until 1935, Gilman wrote "The Yellow Wallpaper," a semiautobiographical story that has become a well-known piece of short fiction. She intended to use the story to expose the detrimental effects of the Weir Mitchell rest cure; in her autobiography, she writes that the real purpose of the story was to convince Mitchell of the error of his ways.[24] She sent him a copy of the story after it was published, but he did not reply. Although there is no evidence to substantiate the rumor, Gilman heard that Mitchell changed his treatment after reading "The Yellow Wallpaper." "If that is a fact," she writes, "I have not lived in vain."[25]

The Weir Mitchell rest cure antedated psychoanalysis and most other psychodynamic approaches, but Gilman was no less critical of these later treatments. She viewed psychoanalysis as a trend rather than as an improvement over other misguided treatments. "Always it has amazed me," she writes, "to see how apparently intelligent persons would permit these mind-meddlers, having no claim to fitness except that of having read certain utterly unproven books, to paddle among their thoughts and feelings, and extract confessions of the last intimacy."[26] As a result of her criticism of psychoanalysis, one psychiatrist sent her a diagnosis and explanation of her own condition. Gilman refused to read it. "Fancy any decent physician," she writes, "presuming to send a diagnosis to some one never his patient, and who on no account would have consulted him!"[27]

Gilman rejected both the conventional treatments for nervous conditions and the new psychological approaches of the early twentieth century. Yet, these new psychotherapies, particularly but not exclusively those of Sigmund Freud, were to have a pervasive effect on the way Americans viewed mental illness and normal psychological development. For patients in large mental hospitals, however, the advent of psychoanalysis made little or no difference. As Dale Peterson writes, "in spite of the impressive publicity surrounding the psychotherapies based on traditional Freudian psychoanalysis, their actual impact on institutional populations has been minor."[28] Institutionalized mental patients were perceived to be suffering from conditions that would not benefit from psychotherapy. Freud believed that psychoanalysis was not an effective treatment for psychosis, although other physicians, such as John Rosen and Frieda Fromm-Reichmann, used psychoanalytic techniques with schizophrenic patients.

Psychoanalysis encouraged individuals to examine their subconscious desires and past experiences for signs of neurosis. Freud's theories pathologized human development in general and women's experiences in particular. As Barbara Ehrenreich and Deirdre English write, "Freud banished the traumatic 'cures' and legitimized a doctor-patient relationship based solely on talking. His therapy urged the patient to confess her resentments and rebelliousness, and then at last to accept her role as a woman."[29] According to Ehrenreich and English, "Psychotherapists found 'rejection of femininity' in every frustrated or unhappy patient."[30] Twentieth-century women's madness narratives illustrate how the approach of a psychiatrist or psychotherapist can shape the way individuals in therapy view their experiences and difficulties. Because of the pervasiveness of sexism in American society, women were particularly vulnerable to the perspectives of their doctors.

Patients' lives had long been of interest to physicians. In 1855 the *Journal of Psychological Medicine and Mental Pathology* published an autobiographical account, which was prefaced by the following statement regarding the importance of such accounts:

> We cannot conceive anything more deeply interesting to the practical physician, so touchingly affecting the philanthropist, or instructive to the speculative metaphysician and medical psychologist, than the account given by those who have recovered from attacks of insanity, or the workings of the mind, and state of their feelings and sensations, during the existence of mental derangement.[31]

With Freud's emphasis on childhood and the unconscious, the investigation of the life of the patient—including, through psychoanalysis, the patient's inner life—became the primary focus of the new science of psychotherapy. By the time Freud delivered his historic lectures at Clark University in 1909, new psychological models were being developed in the United States. According to Wood, "Adolf Meyer's functionalist model continued to dominate American psychology even after Freud's lectures.[32] Meyer rejected the theory of organic causes of mental illness and therefore distinguished mental hygiene from physical hygiene.[33] He also believed that the clues to mental illness could be found by analyzing patients' lives, and his approach gave autobiographies a new place in psychological research.

A different type of madness narrative emerged with the publication of Clifford Beers's *A Mind That Found Itself* in 1908.[34] "Beginning with *A Mind That Found Itself*," writes Wood, autobiographies by former mental patients "began to appear with introductions and addenda by psychologists and psychiatrists who presented the texts as evidence of both their professional ability to cure the patient and the wonders and terrors of mental illness as experienced from the inside."[35] Unlike earlier reformers, such as Elizabeth Packard, Beers "built his career on his admitted history as a former psychotic."[36] His autobiography not only influenced the history of psychology but also served as a model for the type of account that would dominate madness narratives for much of the twentieth century.

Following Beers's autobiography, madness accounts became more confessional and less defiant. Peterson suggests that the primary significance of *A Mind That Found Itself* is its representation of the conditions in mental hospitals in the early twentieth century. He writes, "Beers's direct and vivid accounts of ward life at the turn of the century remain a particularly disturbing reminder of what can happen when people are given almost unlimited power over others." According to Peterson, Beers "wanted to start a patients' rights movement to change the treatment of American mental patients."[37] Instead, Beers helped to found the National Committee for Mental Hygiene, which "did not actually address itself to asylum patients and their injustices on anything more than a token scale."[38] Porter characterizes the shift in Beers's actions as going from "battling against the doctors" to joining them,[39] and the general trajectory of women's madness narratives forms an analogous pattern. In the nineteenth century, most of the women who wrote madness narratives were clearly "battling against the doctors." In the twentieth century, however, women's madness narratives tended to support the psychiatric establishment.

Marian King's *The Recovery of Myself* and Jane Hillyer's *Reluctantly Told* were among the first women's madness narratives written after Beers's autobiography. King's book has a similar title to *A Mind That Found Itself*, and the doctor who introduces Hillyer's narrative begins by praising Beers's autobiography. Adolf Meyer, who worked with Beers to develop mental hygiene organizations, wrote the introduction to King's autobiography, and he praises the book for showing the success of psychiatric treatment. In these autobiographies, the women come to accept the expert opinions of their doctors; moreover, doing so is perceived as an indication of recovery. Meyer's description of King's recovery of *herself* is unintentionally ironic; according to Meyer, King "became socialized, a participant in the hospital world, and finally capable of seeing herself as the physician sees her, with a growing sense of proportion and perspective."[40] Packard, Smith, and Lathrop continually resist the "perspective" of their doctors, but King "finds herself" by seeing herself as her physician saw her.

King, whose narrative was published in 1931, was hospitalized following an overdose of veronal, which she had become at least psychologically dependent upon. She was sent to a private hospital and enjoyed a level of care very different from women who were confined in state institutions. " 'This is supposed to be a Mental and Nervous Hospital,' " another patient tells her. " 'And it is just fortunate that it is a Private Institution where just those that can afford it come.' "[41] According to King, the hospital had athletic facilities and a library, and patients frequently engaged in activities such as tennis, bridge, sewing, and handicrafts. In addition, King had regular sessions with psychiatrists and was also given psychological tests.

King's narrative illustrates the focus on the life of the patient. One of her doctors requires her to tell her life story, which she reproduces in *The Recovery of Myself*. Her treatment also shows the influence of the mental hygiene movement, which was a continuation of earlier forms of moral treatment. Mental health was seen as analogous to medical health, and, like public health programs, mental hygiene approaches stressed prevention and the development or restoration of health-promoting behaviors. King's doctor tells her that "selfishness, wilfulness, and resentment are your chief obstacles. Now fight them off. Conquer them as you have the drug. Let them find a way out of your system—a natural way."[42]

Self-determination and perseverance are traits that are valued in men; however, because King is a woman, these traits constitute mental illness. When she tells a nurse that she is not mentally ill, the nurse contradicts her:

> She told me the reason for saying that I was ill was that if I did not get my own way one way I got it another; said that I was spoiled and, being spoiled as I was, was a mental illness. That I had never had to combat with anything as far as desires were concerned. I knew that I had to combat with a great deal but after all it was in the game.[43]

Before she was admitted to the hospital, King manipulated others by taking small overdoses of veronal. However, she does so because her father decides what she can and cannot do, which disempowers her. Because of the imbalance of power, King must learn how to play the game so that she can get what she wants.

The doctors, like King's father, have power over her; they determine the rules of the game. When a doctor tells King to "fac[e] the facts of [her]self,"[44] he means that she must accept his perspective on her behavior. The doctor is the expert, and there is no room for disagreement between his perspective and hers. Because of the imbalance of power, King must compromise and accept the doctor's opinions of her. Moreover, to do so constitutes mental health. Apparently, King learned how to play the doctor's game, too.

Jane Hillyer's narrative, published in 1926, presents a more negative image of hospitalization and treatment for mental illness. *Reluctantly Told* is reminiscent of nineteenth-century madness narratives because of its portrayal of deception and brutality. When Hillyer is transferred to another hospital, she is led to believe that she is going home. As a result, she finds it hard to trust her new doctor or the other staff members. She is also abused by hospital employees. During her hospitalization, she is injured when a nurse throws a cup back at her, and is severely beaten by a nurse who overhears Hillyer refer to her as a man.

In addition to depicting abusive attendants, Hillyer points out the status of the "underclass" of patients. "The nurses," she writes, "were 'they,' people apart."[45] She describes the practice of having the patients walk nude to the dormitory at bedtime, and comments that "It was easier for the nurses to handle the patients in herds."[46] The doctor puts an end to this practice, and Hillyer comments that it was incredible that such "processions" had ever occurred. "Couldn't even young nurses realize that fragments of people are not necessarily animals?" she asks.[47] Of the institution itself, Hillyer writes that "it was so unnatural, this place where one group had such power over another."[48] Yet, she also writes that the institution "was too monstrous even to permit of protest."[49]

Hillyer determines that doctors and other hospital staff will have as little control over her as possible. After being lied to about going home, she becomes aware of her vulnerability and keeps up her guard. "They had had their one chance," she writes. "[T]hey should not get me under their power."[50] According to Hillyer, the workings of the sanitarium are irrational:

> I could not accommodate myself to a state of things where personal freedom did not exist, and where force was used. Again and again I attacked the problem. Personal responsibility, freedom to make one's own mistakes and profit by them, seemed to me the law of life. . . . I was utterly unprepared for the taking of what seemed to me senseless orders, doing things merely because "the others were." It was not cooperation; it was slavery.[51]

Despite Hillyer's initial questioning of psychiatric power, *Reluctantly Told*, unlike many nineteenth-century madness narratives, focuses on symptoms more than abuses. As Hillyer describes her various symptoms, she sometimes recalls traumatic events in her life. Her narrative strategy implies a connection between her illness and her past experiences. She objectifies her illness as a *"thing"* that takes possession of her.[52] Hillyer perceives herself as being possessed by a disease. Her apparent acceptance of the importance of the past and the reification of symptoms into a disease reflects the influence of psychological theories and the medical model of mental illness. Moreover, Hillyer also comes to accept the perspective of her doctors. Her transition from resistance to submission begins when the doctor visits her, and Hillyer "had one of those curious experiences in which one sees oneself." However, she sees herself from the doctor's perspective; Hillyer writes, "I saw what she saw."[53]

The title of Hillyer's autobiography, *Reluctantly Told*, marks another difference between nineteenth- and twentieth-century madness narratives. Packard, Metcalf, Smith, Lathrop, and Agnew clearly wanted to publish their autobiographies—both for personal vindication and to call for reform—but Hillyer's story is "reluctantly told." She writes, "I was perfectly conscious that the attitude toward insanity was still one of recoil on the part of a large portion of society; it is a disgrace, a thing to speak of in whispers."[54] Despite her reluctance to tell her story, Hillyer decided to write her autobiography so that others would know that there is hope for even severely ill patients.

Influenced by the new emphasis on psychopathology, women's accounts of mental illness and psychiatric treatment became less concerned with asylum reform. Instead of focusing on the rights of women and mental patients, these accounts described the author's "struggle with mental illness," often using the language and concepts of specific disease models and then proclaiming the benefits of particular therapies. Lucy Freeman's *Fight against Fears*,[55] for instance, is an account of her psychoanalysis, and Joanne Greenberg's fictionalized account, *I Never Promised You a Rose Garden*, conceptualizes Deborah Blau's illness in a psychodynamic framework. In these autobiographies, the prison is no longer the asylum but the diseased mind of the mentally ill person. The title of Barbara Field Benziger's autobiography, *The Prison of My Mind*, reveals the change from viewing the asylum as a prison to an understanding of "mental illness" as its own confinement.

In Greenberg's autobiographical novel, *I Never Promised You a Rose Garden* (first published under a pseudonym in 1964), Deborah Blau is confined by the delusional system of her schizophrenic reaction. Through hallucinations and fantasies, Deborah withdraws into "the Kingdom of Yr." *I Never Promised You a Rose Garden* is shaped by the psychological theories of Frieda Fromm-Reichmann, who was Greenberg's psychiatrist. According to Peterson, Deborah's disease process matches Fromm-Reichmann's theoretical concepts. "Fromm-

Reichmann believed that schizophrenia may be caused by un-satisfying or traumatic relationships with parents experienced as an infant," writes Peterson. "Deborah's schizophrenia fits that theoretical pattern very well. It is made clear that her re-lationship with her parents was in some way flawed."[56]

In contrast to Deborah's parents, the Fromm-Reichmann character, Dr. Fried, is portrayed as a saintly physician who gives up professional opportunities and personal pleasures so that she can work with patients. At the same time, however, the novel's point of view allows readers access to Dr. Fried's inner world. She questions the sanity of the world, particularly as she thinks about the attempted genocide of the Jews during World War II. Dr. Fried remembers a patient who returned to the hospital because it was a saner place than the outside world. She tells Deborah's mother about a severely ill patient who recovered, only to die at Dachau. The portrayal of Dr. Fried's thoughts and feelings make her character much more than an infallible, saintly expert.

I Never Promised You a Rose Garden also differs from many accounts of Freudian and post-Freudian therapy because the novel centers on the relationship between a strong and knowl-edgeable woman, Dr. Fried, and a courageous and intelligent young woman, Deborah Blau. As numerous feminist writers have pointed out, Freudian psychology relies heavily on dis-tinctions between the sexes. In Lucy Freeman's account of her psychoanalysis, *Fight against Fears*, the male psychiatrist holds all the power, including the authority to teach Freeman her role as a woman.

In *Fight against Fears*, published in 1951, many of Freeman's difficulties in life are attributed to her failure to assume her proper role as a woman. Through her sessions with her psychi-atrist, whom she calls John, Freeman "faces" her unhappy childhood, her attempts to please her parents by "being" a boy, and her desire for her father. "I had been trying to deny my childhood," she writes. "I had to accept it so I could stop living in the first years of my life."[57] A major part of her troubles stemmed from her supposed sex-role confusion:

> I scorned dolls, believing my parents preferred me, the first-born, to be a boy. I was not sure whether I was supposed to be a boy or girl and eternal warfare raged within—nature versus the pull of

parents. I tried to make myself believe I was "a good girl" all my life, but I never believed I was good nor was I sure I was a girl.[58]

During Freeman's psychoanalysis, children's behavior and adult roles are sex-typed by her therapist. Adherence to pre-scribed sex roles, such as playing with toys that are judged to be appropriate for one's sex, is perceived as a mark of normal development. John pathologizes Freeman's rejection of her gender role, which is indicated in her adult life by her career as a journalist, her dislike of domestic duties, and her status as an independent woman. What would be viewed as healthy behavior for men is a sign of pathology in women. Although society itself values the characteristics associated with men, it is considered abnormal for women to value these traits in themselves. "I was doomed by my own fantasy of being a boy to pursue a career," writes Freeman. "I felt I must be some-body, that no one could possibly like me unless I proved my worth."[59]

As a result of her psychoanalysis, Freeman's "Feminine feel-ings seeped to the surface."[60] She decides that her "scorn for women whose lives revolved around dishes and babies was sheer envy."[61] She comes to view her career as a substitute for romantic involvement with men. Freeman writes, "I said to John wistfully, 'I'd like to be like the other girls.' "[62] *Fight against Fears* is a poignant example of how psychotherapy can be used against women in patriarchal society. The fear being fought seems to be the fear of independent women. Freeman's problems could be understood to stem from the constraints placed on women. It is significant that Freeman's sessions with John began immediately after World War II, a time in which women were expected to have babies instead of a career. A final indication of Freeman's internalization of the oppression of the therapeutic enforcement of sex roles is the way she en-dorses psychoanalysis and its exorbitant fees:

It took a long time to know that if I had an unhappy childhood the only way I would get happiness was by paying for it, just as I paid for all else I lacked and desired. . . . I had to pay for a skill known as psychoanalysis, combination art and science, that would give me a chance to face myself. . . . It was expensive but all the money in the world could not pay for what it brought me—peace of mind.[63]

For Freeman, psychoanalysis was priceless; however, her therapy can also be seen as a series of remedial lessons in femininity that cost Freeman dearly.

Lenore McCall's *Between Us and the Dark*,[64] which was contemporaneous with *Fight against Fears*, also depicts the miracles of the developing science of psychiatry and the impact of sex-role stereotyping on treatment. McCall's doctor, C. Charles Burlingame, describes her successful course of treatment in the introduction to *Between Us and the Dark*. Burlingame italicizes the names of McCall's treatments, including shock therapies, physical rebuilding, and reeducational therapy, giving the impression that medical advances are more important than McCall herself. For Burlingame, the success of McCall's therapy justifies her narrative. "In my opinion," he writes, "[McCall's] manuscript is destined to be a lasting contribution to the further liquidation of the unjustified pessimism and fear surrounding mental illness."[65] At the same time, *Between Us and the Dark* also functions as an advertisement for the Institute of Living, where Burlingame was chief of staff.

After describing McCall's treatment, Burlingame mentions the "delicate process of re-education and rehabilitation" that followed her recovery. This process included "reintroducing her to domestic problems and relationships," and was complete when McCall "establish[ed] herself in a well-rounded program of activities at the Institute [of Living] which corresponded to those in her daily life at home."[66] McCall's recovery supposedly depends on her acceptance of domestic responsibilities; however, feminine roles are socially constructed and should not be viewed as indicative of mental health. Moreover, as the foregoing analysis has shown, traditionally feminine duties perpetuated Gilman's difficulties, and Packard, Smith, Lathrop, and Agnew had problematic—if not unhealthy—family relationships.

Benziger's narrative, which was published in 1969, is aptly titled *The Prison of My Mind*. *The Prison of My Mind* illustrates the focus on psychopathology and the internalization of social constraints. "I am locking myself up in a prison of my own making, a horrible, painful prison, to which I have no key," she writes. "Someone must help me—save me from myself."[67] According to Benziger, only her psychiatrist has the keys to unlock the prison. " '[Y]ou made me well,' " she tells him. " 'You gave me keys to all kinds of new doors that I knew were there all along, but I couldn't find the keys to unlock them.' "[68] Benziger gives up her power and submits to the authority of her psychiatrist. It is the psychiatrist who tells her that she must divorce her husband to regain her mental health. Benziger's interpretation of the psychotherapeutic process negates her own agency throughout her treatment. The divorce is practically a prescription in which one man (the doctor) sanctions her independence from another (her first husband).

The Prison of My Mind contains many of the elements commonly found in madness narratives written by women between 1920 and 1970. Benziger dedicates the book "to the doctor who made we well, and . . . my husband." Her book is introduced by a psychiatrist, Robert Coles, who explicitly links Benziger's narrative to *A Mind That Found Itself*. Sixty years after its publication, Beers's narrative remains the standard autobiography of a recovered mental patient. The only other account of madness referred to in Coles's introduction is *I Never Promised You a Rose Garden*. As is the case with many other madness narratives of the twentieth century, Benziger's stated purpose for writing is to give others hope. "If I can help others to realize the depth to which the human spirit can sink, and the heights to which it can rise again," she writes, "my story will have been worth the telling."[69]

Benziger also writes to fight the effects of the illness—unlike Elizabeth Packard, who kept a journal to maintain her sense of self despite her confinement. Rather than asserting her sense of reality in the face of oppression, Benziger keeps a journal "in a desperate attempt to hang on to some shred of reality and sanity"[70] in the prison of mental illness. She also struggles to understand what she considers to be a mental disease. "I *had* to understand this eclipse of the mind."[71] She distinguishes between understanding and knowledge, however. "I felt I must contribute my small measure toward a better understanding—not so much knowledge, but understanding."[72] Knowledge, whether self-knowledge or psychological expertise, is reserved for trained professionals.

Benziger portrays herself as a passive victim of mental illness. She reports that "suicidal thoughts *set in*,"[73] describing her symptoms in terms typically reserved for medical conditions (for instance, one might say that gangrene "set in"). Her medical metaphors reveal her acceptance of the medical model of "mental illness." She complains of crippling emotions and is relieved that she won't be "semi-crippled by emotions" for the rest of her life.[74] As she describes her "broken and tormented mind," which is "contained" within her body, the isolation she experiences is caused by an illness and the "dungeon" is her mind.[75]

Benziger neither doubts her own need for treatment nor questions the hospitalization of other patients. Therefore, she makes no distinction between mentally ill and mentally healthy inpatients, although she does judge the severity of her illness relative to other patients. For the most part, however, her distinctions are based on other factors, primarily social class. Benziger, an economically privileged white woman, sees herself as different from the poorer patients at the "bad hospital." Unlike the narratives of the previous century, Benziger does not write about other women patients; her life and her story are clearly separated from theirs. Nor does she advocate for improved conditions in mental hospitals; although she objects to her treatment at the first hospital ("the bad hospital"), she asserts, "I am not intimating, even remotely, that I went through any 'snake-pit' experience."[76]

Psychodynamic approaches constitute the dominant mode of treatment in twentieth-century women's madness narratives. Most of these reflect post-Freudian psychoanalysis, although other forms of treatment are also presented, particularly those that follow the medical model of disease. In addition to psychoanalysis and other forms of psychotherapy, physically oriented treatments, such as cold packs, various shock therapies, and psychosurgery (i.e., lobotomy and leucotomy), also play a role in twentieth-century narratives. Descriptions of electroshock therapy are particularly common in accounts from the mid–twentieth century. Esther Greenwood, the protagonist of Sylvia Plath's autobiographical novel, *The Bell Jar*, benefits from shock treatment. Electroconvulsive therapy (ECT) is especially prominent in accounts of depression, such as Benziger's narrative, although the autobiographies of schizophrenics also describe shock treatments. New Zealand writer Janet Frame, diagnosed as schizophrenic, received ECT and was even on the "lobotomy list," although she never underwent psychosurgery. Recent accounts show the continued prominence of the medical model by depicting recovery after treatment with psychotropic medication, megavitamin therapy, and dialysis.

Greenberg's novel, *I Never Promised You a Rose Garden*, illustrates the trend toward anonymity, which involved using a pseudonym and publishing a largely autobiographical account as a work of fiction. In addition to its presentation as a novel, *I Never Promised You a Rose Garden* was originally published under a pseudonym, and Sylvia Plath used a pseudonym when she wrote *The Bell Jar*. The publication of fictionalized and pseudonymous accounts can be related to the emphasis on psychopathology over against exposés of psychiatric treatment. Writers who are intent on exposing the horrors of forced institutionalization do not need to hide their identity (although Mary Jane Ward did so in her semiautobiographical novel, *The Snake Pit*, which popularized the image of the mental hospital reflected in the book's title). Using their actual names gives credence to their accounts (as women who have experienced forced hospitalization); moreover, if they are trying to vindicate themselves through these accounts, it is imperative that their identity be known. On the other hand, writers who portray themselves as mentally ill, even if they have recovered, may feel the need to hide their identity. Anonymity is one way of avoiding the stigma of mental disease.

Another trend that reflects the twentieth-century emphasis on pathology is the presentation of autobiographical writings as case studies. Instead of simply providing a frame for a patient's autobiography, the case presentation format allows the author, who is someone other than the patient, to control the narrative. The case presentation format is particularly useful when the patient does not recover. Without a successful case to offer a firsthand account of the miracles of psychiatric treatment, autobiographical writings can still be used to advance particular theories of mental illness. Two examples of this approach, both published in the United States in the 1950s, are *Autobiography of a Schizophrenic Girl* and "The Case of Ellen West."[77] *Autobiography of a Schizophrenic Girl* consists of the first-person narrative of "Renee," a "schizophrenic girl," and "expert" commentary by her psychiatrist, Marguerite Sechehaye. *Autobiography of a Schizophrenic Girl* recounts a successful "case," whereas the subject of "The Case of Ellen West" committed suicide. Both of these case studies include autobiographical accounts that have been appropriated and published by psychiatrists. Psychiatric literature cites cases as a matter of course, and the analysis of Ellen West's anorexia is contained in a psychology text; however, *Autobiography of a Schizophrenic Girl* was eventually published in the United States as a mass market paperback rather than as a psychiatric text.

Although titled (or, as in the original English translation, subtitled) *Autobiography of a Schizophrenic Girl*, Grace Rubin-Rabson, the translator of the book, asserts that it is superior to an autobiography. "Personal retrospections of mental illness during periods of remission or recovery are not rare in either popular or psychiatric literature," writes Rubin-Rabson. "Too often the rampant overdramatization, the search for appealing literary devices, the defects in recall and the confusion in sequence rob the reporting of scientific value." In *Autobiography of a Schizophrenic Girl*, "the retrospections were under control."[78] Despite the psychiatrist's control over the narrative, sales of *Autobiography of a Schizophrenic Girl* indicate that the book appealed to the public and not just to mental health professionals and students.

The popularity of books such as *Autobiography of a Schizophrenic Girl* indicates the continuing attraction of sensational literature by or about the "mentally ill." However, in the twentieth century, sensational accounts of psychopathology, especially multiple personality disorder, have replaced the prior century's sensational exposés of psychiatric abuse. The cover of the paperback edition of Flora Rheta Schreiber's *Sybil* proclaims that the book contains "The true and extraordinary story of a woman possessed by sixteen separate personalities."[79] Some of these sensational accounts, such as *Sybil* and *The Three Faces of Eve*,[80] fall under the rubric of biographies or case studies. *I'm Eve*,[81] on the other hand, purports to be an autobiographical account by the woman whose story was the basis for *The Three Faces of Eve*. In the introductory material, which includes a foreword by a psychiatrist and a preface by the book's coauthor, Elen Sain Pittillo, Chris Costner Sizemore explains her reasons for telling her version of the story. Sizemore hopes that the book will help people "better understand and accept the mentally disturbed" and provide hope for those who need it. In addition, there are some indications that *I'm Eve* is an attempt to outdo *Sybil* in number of personalities and, correspondingly, in sales. Sizemore writes,

> This book was born because of my conviction that the true facts of my life were not known, and that I had a story to tell; because the world had the impression that I had recovered from my dissociative problem, multiple personality. I have known twenty-two personalities and have lived to tell of their demise.

I'm Eve, writes Sizemore, "is my life as I have lived it. These are my memories and impressions," she writes, "and my emotions."[82] Oddly enough, however, the book is not only coauthored but also uses third-person point of view in most of the narrative.

In addition to *I'm Eve*, which was published in 1977, several other autobiographical accounts of multiple personality disorder (now referred to as dissociative identity disorder) have been published since *Sybil*, which seems to have firmly established the subgenre of writings by and about "multiples." The book even influenced the diagnostic category itself. As Mikkel Borch-Jacobsen writes, "Multiple Personality Disorder (or MPD, as it is known to psychiatrists) was born in 1973 with the publication of Flora Rheta Schreiber's book *Sybil*."[83] Although *Sybil* was not the first such narrative, its success created a market for books about multiple personality disorder. Accounts of multiple personality disorder often have sensational titles, such as *Katherine, It's Time: The Incredible True Story of the Multiple Personalities of Kit Castle* and *Murderous Memories: One Woman's Hellish Battle to Save Herself*.[84] The sensational elements of these accounts have caused many people to be skeptical of the narratives as well as of the diagnostic category of multiple personality disorder.

Herbert Spiegel, a psychiatrist who worked with "Sybil," maintains that her story was misrepresented so that it would be a sensational bestseller. Spiegel apparently refused to collaborate with Schreiber and Sybil's psychiatrist, Cornelia Wilbur. In an interview with Borch-Jacobsen, Spiegel claimed that Schreiber became upset with him when he asserted that Sybil was not a multiple personality. "[I]f we don't call it a multiple personality, we don't have a book!" Schreiber apparently told Spiegel. "The publishers want it to be that, otherwise it won't sell!" According to Spiegel, "That was the logic behind their calling Sybil a multiple personality."[85] Regardless of the intent, Sybil's story differs from subsequent accounts because it was written by a journalist. The majority of narratives of multiple personality disorder have been written by women who claim to have MPD.

One of the most fascinating examples of appropriation is Lara Jefferson's *These Are My Sisters*, first published in 1947 (Lara Jefferson is a pseudonym).[86] Jefferson, a patient on a disturbed ward in a state hospital, was writing an account of her experiences on various scraps of paper. When Jefferson's doctor became aware of what she was doing, he provided her with proper materials and encouraged her to keep writing. According to Bert Kaplan, Jefferson's physician sent her manuscript to Jack Vickers, a publisher, and Jefferson allowed it to be published. Like Hillyer, King, and Benziger, Jefferson dedicated the book to her doctor. She dedicates the book "To the 'mental surgeon' responsible for my rebirth. During my bloodless 'insandectomy' he removed egotism—and left endurance."[87] Her dedication reflects the medical model of mental illness and praises the expertise of the psychiatrist, a skillful surgeon who performs a successful "insandectomy."

In his introduction to *These Are My Sisters*, Vickers makes the composition and publication of the book sound mysterious; he even states that the author is "unavailable" to write a preface. "Mr. Vickers has done a superb job of editing," writes Kaplan, "spending more than six months sorting and arranging the materials." Kaplan suggests that the edited manuscript "is probably a more coherent and organized manuscript than Miss Jefferson wrote."[88] In his introduction, Vickers praises the book because "nowhere is any crusading, any preachments, any 'pointing with pride' or 'viewing with alarm' carried on."[89] As the editor and publisher of the manuscript, Vickers determined the form of Jefferson's narrative, and it seems that she had little or no control over the publication process. The publication history of *These Are My Sisters* shows that psychological theories of the twentieth century not only oppressed women in society but also disempowered them as writers.

In contrast to the rebellious narratives of the nineteenth century, many twentieth-century madness narratives are confessional in tone and politically regressive in content. The women who decided to tell their stories emphasize their helplessness in the face of mental disease and the expertise of doctors who cure them. The passive vulnerability of incarcerated women is more apparent in books that are appropriated by doctors, publishers, journalists, and even friends and relatives. In these works, the women are thoroughly disempowered; they are presented as unable to tell their life stories properly. Their helplessness in regard to their condition and its treatment is perpetuated as doctors and others present the narrative to the public. The absolute power of the physician and of psychiatric discourse itself precludes rebellion and, in some cases, the agency of authorship. In these narratives, the women are not only unable to become the heroes of their own lives, but are also barred from providing the interpretative frame for their narratives. In some cases, they are not even allowed to tell their own stories. In many ways the prison of the mind was stronger than the walls of an insane asylum.

4

Questioning Psychiatric Power: Mary Jane Ward, Susanna Kaysen, Jill Johnston, and Kate Millett

In GENERAL, THE WRITERS OF THE NARRATIVES DISCUSSED IN chapter 3 accepted their diagnoses and the therapeutic interventions of psychiatric "experts." At the same time, however, their narratives also criticize aspects of psychiatric practice. For instance, although Hillyer expresses extreme gratitude toward the doctors who worked with her, she also depicts abusive and degrading treatment of patients. Similarly, the emphasis on the relationship between doctor and patient in *I Never Promised You a Rose Garden* can be seen as an implicit criticism of nonnurturing relationships, particularly those structured by medical treatments, such as shock therapies and psychotropic medications.

During the period characterized by women's acceptance of psychopathology, Mary Jane Ward's semiautobiographical novel, *The Snake Pit*, which was first published in 1946, stands out for its criticism of psychiatric treatment.[1] *The Snake Pit* is also significant because Ward draws upon the techniques available to the novelist to make her points about psychiatric care. Moreover, the book's criticism of psychiatric practice is embedded in the very structure of the narrative. The point of view, although always focused on the experiences of the protagonist, Virginia Cunningham, shifts constantly; the reader can never be confident of the "correct" perspective. The use of second-person point of view functions to draw the reader into Virginia's experience of psychiatric hospitalization. On the one hand, the use of second-person pronouns represents an informal speech style and could be said to maintain the first-person point of view. However, the frequent interpolation of second-person pronouns can have a cumulative effect in which the reader moves from the position of spectator into the role of institutionalized mental patient.

The relative positions of reader, character, and narrator are ambiguous from the beginning of the novel. In the opening line, " 'Do you hear voices?' he asked," it is unclear who is speaking, why he asks about voices, and who is being addressed. The character being addressed is also confused by the question:

> You think I am deaf? "Of course," she said. "I hear yours." It was hard to keep on being civil. She was tired and he had been asking questions such a long time, days and days of incredibly naïve questions.
> Now he was explaining that she misunderstood; he did not mean real voices. Fantastic. He was speaking, he said, of voices that were not and yet they were voices he expected her to hear. He seemed determined that she should hear them. He was something of a pest, this man, but she could think of no decent way to get rid of him. You could tell he meant well and so you tried to play the game with him, as if with a fanciful child.
> "You can make water say anything," she said. That should appeal to the childish fancy that leaped from pebble to pebble, dancing in the sun, giggling in the sparkle.[2]

From the beginning, *The Snake Pit* problematizes the easy bifurcation of sanity and insanity. The behavior of the unnamed person, who turns out to be the doctor, is presented as childish and nonsensical. His speech is described as "gibberish," a word that is often used in relation to people who are identified as insane or "feeble-minded":

> For once he was not asking questions; he was letting gibberish flow from his lips and you would have far more difficulty making sense from it than you would have in imagining words from a genuine stream. Suppose it was not he.
> She turned her head. He had a peculiar habit of crouching behind you. Was he in the bushes? And just who was he?[3]

This incident is explained near the end of the book in a conversation between Virginia and her husband, Robert. Robert tells Virginia that she had been psychoanalyzed during her hospital stay. Virginia is surprised; "You mean he psychoanalyzed me?" she asks. "You mean when he was hiding some-where in the bushes and asking those silly questions about did I hear voices. . . . It's sort of vague now."[4] Robert criticizes the doctor and his therapeutic technique. "Maybe he's right according to a book of theories," he tells Virginia, "but he still doesn't know you."[5] Remembering the black couch, Virginia says, "I don't think it's fair to ask a person questions when the person doesn't know what's going on."[6] Robert and Virginia criticize the doctor's approach because he "doesn't know his patient" and even "hides" from her. They portray his therapy as a form of hit-and-run; the patient, Virginia, is taken by surprise in an interaction in which she alone is vulnerable.

The critique of psychoanalysis is strategically placed. During the first part of the novel, readers are likely to dismiss incidents such as the opening portrayal of the interview with Dr. Kik as indications of Virginia's "mental illness." As the novel progresses, readers are more likely to empathize with Virginia and her situation. Furthermore, the novel draws readers into the narrative. *The Snake Pit* mimetically represents the experience of hospitalization, and, as the novel develops, readers may even identify with Virginia and enter into her experience.

The Snake Pit transports readers into a surreal world where nothing makes sense. Instead of describing the nonsensical rules and abusive practices of the institution, Ward takes readers into the irrational world of the hospital, "Juniper Hill." Virginia describes Juniper Hill as "barren" and says that the "overpowering" smell of paraldehyde pervades the wards.[7] As Albert Deutsch points out, Juniper Hill is based on Rockland State Hospital in New York. When Deutsch visited Rockland in the 1940s, he observed both overcrowding and under-staffing. The hospital housed 6,100 patients in buildings intended for 4,700, and needed "twice as many doctors, twice as many nurses, and three times as many attendants."[8] Yet, despite major deficiencies in living conditions and medical treatment, Deutsch refers to Rockland as one of the best state hospitals in New York State.[9]

The novel allows—or perhaps forces—readers to experience Virginia's confusion and powerlessness. As a mental patient, Virginia has no autonomy. She is transferred from ward to ward, all of which have identical layouts and are distinguished mainly by number and the apparent degree of illness among the patients. Like the other patients, she is clothed in numbered garments, and the number is changed with each transfer. Virginia's memory is clouded by electroshock amnesia, and, as she wanders through the haze, it is possible that her confusion stems from a combination of the effects of shock treatments and her confinement in the unreal environment of Juniper Hill.

On the surface, it appears as if *The Snake Pit* does not question Virginia's illness as much as the way she is treated. Yet, the snake pit is not the experience of "mental illness" but the institution itself. The quotation that precedes the title page of *The Snake Pit* aptly conveys the perspective of the book: "Long ago they lowered insane persons into snake pits; they thought that an experience that might drive a sane person out of his wits might send an insane person back into sanity."[10] The passage occurs later in the novel, where it is introduced in reference to shock treatments. "Why bother with insulin, metrazol or electricity?"[11] The narrative implies that modern psychiatric treatment has not advanced beyond the snake pit.

Although Virginia refers to herself as "a woman who is not sane,"[12] she does not describe herself as a prisoner of her own diseased mind. As in the madness narratives of the nineteenth century, Ward depicts the institution or "snake pit" as a prison and the perceived "illness" as a crime. When Virginia is told in August that she had been in the hospital since February, she thinks, "Was my crime so great?"[13] The hospital staff are at times referred to as "guards," as is the case when the medication procedure is described: "The guard poured something into a lilycup and the prisoner drank it down. While the prisoner choked and sputtered the guard refilled the cup from another pitcher and this was drunk gratefully."[14] In addition, Virginia refers to her doctor as "the Indefatigable Examiner,"[15] and just as she rejects psychoanalysis as "gibberish," Virginia compares shock treatments to electrocution:

> They put a wedge under her back. It was most uncomfortable. It forced her back into an unnatural position. She looked at the dull glass eye that was set into the wall and she knew that soon it would glow and that she would not see the glow. They were going to electrocute her. . . . Even now the woman was applying a sort of foul-smelling cold paste to your temples. What had you done? You wouldn't have killed anyone and what other crime is there which exacts so severe a penalty?[16]

According to the perspective of *The Snake Pit*, however, seeing oneself as a prisoner does not depend on seeing others as insane and asserting one's own sanity. Yet, many of Virginia's thoughts about her "illness" are ambiguous. At one point, for instance, she rejects the language of prisons and crimes as an attempt to "glamorize" her experience. "Around you in the washroom were women who were shut up with you, women who were more wretched than criminals," she thinks. "What it is, is the one thing I can not take. I could face the prospect of blindness, of cancer, but this, no. Never this."[17] Because of the use of unclear referents such as "it" and "this," Virginia could be referring to her illness, the illness of those around her, the conditions of the hospital, or some combination of these things. Other times the focus is more clearly the hospital, as when the narrator tells us, "All along [Virginia] had known where she was, but she had invented a setting that was easier to endure." Virginia's thoughts immediately follow this statement as the point of view switches to first person. "I knew, I knew," she thinks, "but I tried to close the door on my knowing."[18]

Virginia often uses metaphors and plays with language. Laying bare "the prison fantasy," the narrator reveals that "All along [Virginia] had known that the electrocution and crime idea was nonsense. All along she had known where she was. Oh, she did not know the geography of it, but she knew, she knew."[19] The use of the word *geography* here is particularly interesting, because one of Virginia's frustrations is that the wards are identical in layout. They can only be distinguished by number, personnel, and perhaps by the behavior of the patients. The transfers from ward to ward are disorienting to Virginia, and even when she remains on a ward for a period of time she is often confused by the way she is moved around without knowing where she is going or why she must go there.

As her stay in the hospital continues, she realizes that normal reality is suspended or lost in mental institutions. "They took the night away from you," writes the narrator. "They drugged you and put you to bed before dark."[20] Virginia cannot keep track of the current day, month, or year because she is never told such information. Moreover, she finds that time is different at Juniper Hill; "sometimes it was long and sometimes it was short and sometimes—this was disconcerting—it was not at all."[21] The point of view then changes to the second person:

> In real life you had been able to count on time; you might feel you hadn't enough of it, but it was always there, nicely parceled out in seconds and minutes and hours. Each day had twenty-four hours and you were able to depend on tomorrow. As with the stars it was something you took for granted. But here, here in the world of Juniper Hill, a day might consist of weeks, of hours. Of a minute, or, frighteningly, of not even a second.[22]

Time is also disrupted by irrational schedules and unnecessary hurrying. Patients are told to race down the tunnel to the cafeteria for meals. Before Virginia can finish eating at a reasonable pace, the patients are told to leave the dining room and once again race through the tunnel to the ward. Yet, when they are back on the ward, there are no activities to occupy them. They have been rushed to and from their meals only to pass time in the dayroom. The time-consciousness that surrounds meals is contrived by the hospital staff; despite the pretense of important schedules, every moment at Juniper is "insufferably dull."[23]

Unlike the autobiographies of the nineteenth century, the structure of Ward's narrative questions the notion of a simple bifurcation of sanity and insanity. The pathologizing of Virginia's behavior is dependent on viewing her as mentally ill. Yet, as David Rosenhan argues in "On Being Sane in Insane Places," the assumptions about the relative sanity of an individual influence how he or she is evaluated. The article summarizes a famous experiment of the early 1970s, in which eight "normal" people, including Rosenhan himself, falsely reported having hallucinations so that they could be admitted to psychiatric hospitals. Once admitted, these pseudopatients made no attempt to simulate mental illness, yet they were never detected as "sane" impostors. The experimenters then attempted to determine whether the tendency to perceive "sane" people as "insane" could be reversed. The staff at a research and teaching hospital was falsely informed that at least one pseudopatient would attempt to be admitted to the psychiatric ward. Of 193 patients, 41 of them were judged to be pseudopatients by at least one member of the hospital staff. Based on the results of these studies, Rosenhan concludes, "we cannot distinguish the sane from the insane in psychiatric hospitals."[24]

Similarly, *"sanity or psychosis,"* writes R. D. Laing, *"is tested by the degree of conjunction or disjunction between two persons where the one is sane by common consent."*[25] According to Laing, the behavior of doctors and other people who are considered sane is unquestioned—at least in regard to those diagnosed as mentally ill, whose behavior is always suspect. Laing provides a poignant example of a case presentation by Emil Kraepelin from the early twentieth century to illustrate the unqualified acceptance of the physician's behavior. The patient, a young woman from the servant class, resists every attempt to interfere with her behavior:

> *On attempting to stop her movement,* we meet with unexpectedly strong resistance; *if I place myself in front of her with my arms spread out* in order to stop her, if she cannot push me on one side, she suddenly turns and slips through under my arms, so as to continue her way. *If one takes firm hold* of her, she distorts her usually rigid, expressionless features with deplorable weeping, that only ceases so soon as one lets her have her own way. . . . The patient does not trouble in the least about her surroundings so long as you leave her alone. *If you prick her in the forehead with a needle,* she scarcely winces or turns away, and leaves the needle quietly sticking there without letting it disturb her restless, bird-of-prey-like wandering backwards and forwards.[26]

"If we see the situation purely in terms of Kraepelin's point of view, it all immediately falls into place," writes Laing. "He is sane, she is insane; he is rational, she is irrational."[27] To do this, however, one must ignore the experience of the patient and the context of her behavior. If, on the other hand, we take Kraepelin's actions "out of the context of the situation as experienced and defined by him, how extraordinary *they* are!"[28]

Generalizing from Kraepelin's example, Laing writes:

> A feature of the interplay between psychiatrist and patient is that if the patient's part is taken out of context, as is done in the clinical description, it might seem very odd. The psychiatrist's part, however, is taken as the very touchstone for our common-sense view of normality. The psychiatrist, as *ipso facto* sane, shows that the patient is out of contact with him. The fact that he is out of contact

with the patient shows that there is something wrong with the patient, but not with the psychiatrist.[29]

One of the necessary shifts for Laing is to "[cease] to identify with the clinical posture and [look] at the psychiatrist-patient couple without such presuppositions."[30] *The Snake Pit* encourages such a shift through the novel's narrative technique and Virginia's rejection of the perspective of the doctors and other hospital staff.

Although not as striking as Laing's example, Virginia's first appearance at "staff" illustrates the importance of distinguishing between the "sane" doctor and the "insane" patient. During "staff," patients are interviewed by a physician in front of an audience of professionals. The interaction reveals the doctor's inability to relate to Virginia:

"Your husband has been here to see you?" Asked the little man.
"Yes."
"How often does he come?"
"As often as the rule allows."
"How often is that?"
She looked at him in surprise. "Why, don't you know?"
There was a sound from the audience; the little man turned around for a moment. "Mrs. Cunningham," he said crossly, as if irritated by her getting a laugh he should have had, "I know. I know all about it. I am simply trying to find out if you know."
"I can't see what difference it makes. Would you change the rule?"
"How often are you allowed to have visitors, Mrs. Cunningham? Will you please answer the questions? It will make it easier for all of us."[31]

When Virginia presents accurate and even sophisticated information, her answers are still seen as indications of pathology:

"I understand you were distressed to be without your glasses," he said.
"I am very nearsighted."
"Yes?"
This meant give further information. "Minus five point seven five minus point twenty-five . . . five. That's the right. Minus five point. . . ."
"What are you talking about?"

"I thought you wanted my prescription."

"That will not be necessary. Have you had your lenses changed recently?"

"Not for several years."

"How do you explain the fact that you remember a rather involved and lengthy prescription when you can't remember your home address?"[32]

If the doctor is not viewed as the standard of sanity, his questions could be seen as meaningless or even irrational. From Virginia's perspective, the doctor's questions are pointless and nonsensical.

The descriptions of the conditions at Juniper Hill reinforce the image of the mental hospital as a snake pit. There are never enough chairs in the dayroom, and patients are forced to sit or lie on the floor. Patients' belongings are treated as communal property. When a group of patients is to be taken outside, the nurse dumps a bunch of coats on the floor of the dayroom. Virginia, unable to find her own coat, is forced to wear whichever coat is left. It turns out to be an ill-fitting men's jacket with a substance resembling dried gravy on the front of it. Just as there is no respect for patients' dignity or belongings, there is also no privacy for the patients. Neither the dormitories nor the bathroom stalls have doors. Even a private shower was nearly impossible.

> You bathed twice a week. You lined up for the showers. There were two stalls for the forty or fifty women who lived in Ward Three and in order to speed things up you were told to soap yourself before you got under the water. You reached a hand into the spray and caught enough moisture for a lather and in that way you could spend your bath time in rinsing. You might almost get completely rinsed before the nurse would tell you to get out. Virginia had not, as yet, ever had a shower stall to herself even for a moment but she understood that this could happen. It was indeed rarely that she had only one other woman in her bath.[33]

Nurses dispense toilet paper as well as soap.

> If you required paper you asked her for it in advance and she doled it out to you. She was the judge of how much you needed. It was a curious and humiliating procedure. Hadn't they gone deep enough

into a woman's privacy when they removed the doors from the booths?[34]

Many of the situations portrayed in *The Snake Pit* could be described as "curious and humiliating."

During one of her work shifts at the hospital—patients did much of the menial labor at state hospitals until the reforms of 1960s and 1970s—Virginia comes upon an unlocked bathroom door. At first, she is taken by the scented soap, a roll of toilet paper on a chromium fixture, and a stack of towels next to the sink. The most important aspect of her discovery, however, is that she could have a few minutes to herself. "I'll just sit here a few minutes and enjoy being alone," Virginia tells herself. "It had been a long time since she had been alone."[35] When the nurses determine that Virginia has shut herself in the bathroom, they coax her out by telling her that her husband has come to visit her. She runs into the dayroom but cannot find her husband. At this point, the point of view switches to the third person:

> They caught her, of course. Someone tripped her and she fell. Instantly her head was encased in a sack and someone was sitting on her legs. The sack was bound tightly around her chest and she could not breathe.[36]

Just as Virginia is powerless against the hospital staff, her voice disappears from the narrative. She is described as a passive object, totally under the control of her captors.

Moreover, Virginia's attempt to enjoy a brief time of privacy is severely punished. As a result of her respite from the constant surveillance of the hospital staff, she is restrained in cold wet cloths and is tied down so tightly that she can do no more than wiggle her toes and her fingers. After a while Virginia figures out how to get out of the restraints so that she can sleep; however, she ends the regime of the nightly wrap not by escaping the restraints but by simply wandering off and finding a dry bed. The nurses have too many patients to restrain at night, and they are relieved to have one less patient to wrap. Similarly, Robert engineers Virginia's release by working the system. He finds the way almost by accident; as he tells Virginia, "I just happened to mention that we'd be going back home and did they perk up!" he tells Virginia. "I've been harping on that ever since." When Virginia asks him why it would matter if they left New York, Robert "laughed as if he had a delicious joke on the dignitaries of Juniper Hill." As he explains, " 'You'd be in another state and they wouldn't be responsible for you any more. They like that.' "[37]

Ward's novel depicts the irrational behavior of the doctors and other staff members at Juniper Hill. The bizarre behavior of the patients sometimes makes sense, while the staff members, who seem to be out of touch with the patients, unquestioningly follow dehumanizing rules, sometimes in a sadistic manner. In the irrational world of *The Snake Pit*, the major difference between patients and staff is that the patients are considered insane, which gives the staff control over them. Sanity and incarceration are questions of power; only those in power can decide that people are insane and determine who should be institutionalized. As a nurse says at the end of novel, " 'I'll tell you where it's going to end. When there's more sick ones than well ones, by golly the sick ones will lock the well ones up.' "[38] Because sanity/insanity cannot be separated from power/powerlessness, designations like "mentally ill" and "in need of treatment" are, to some extent, arbitrary. Those with the power to diagnose and commit others decide who is sane and who is not.

The Snake Pit can also lead readers to question the sanity of their own experiences. Just as the trip into the snake pit was aimed to shock people back to their senses, readers who truly enter the world of *The Snake Pit* might begin to see the irrationality of the world outside the mental hospital. Without negating the suffering and powerlessness of institutionalized mental patients, the mental hospital can serve as a metaphor for an insane world. Although people believe that they are autonomous and that their choices make sense, they may actually be trapped in an irrational world. The capacity for madness narratives to inform perceptions about society is a significant discovery. As chapter 5 of the present study will show, Bessie Head uses a madness narrative to address personal and societal evils. Madness can be located in other places besides the mind of a "mentally ill" individual or an irrational hospital environment like Juniper Hill.

The Snake Pit marks a significant point in the shift from focusing on psychopathology to questioning the rhetoric of madness and psychiatric practice. Eventually, the transition that is apparent in Ward's novel would extend beyond the reform efforts of nineteenth-century women's madness narratives. Although Packard, Metcalf, Smith, and Lathrop were advocating necessary changes in commitment procedures and institutional practices, they maintained the distinction between sane and insane individuals. Their narratives focus on wrongful commitment of sane persons and abusive treatment of institutionalized patients. The need for insane persons to be hospitalized was not questioned; instead, these narratives exposed abusive conditions and argued that psychiatric patients must be cared for with compassion. Writers of nineteenth-century madness narratives were interested in improving the existing system. They were reformers, not revolutionaries.

Because of the impulse toward reform in nineteenth-century madness narratives, there is continuity between nineteenth- and twentieth-century madness narratives. Despite their differences, most of these narratives share the assumptions that it is possible to distinguish the sane from the insane, and that those in need of care should be hospitalized if their problems cannot be managed by outpatient treatment. Nineteenth-century madness narratives actually paved the way for autobiographies such as *The Prison of My Mind*. When women decided that they were, in fact, suffering from "mental illness," they either sought the advice of expert physicians or later credited their recovery to hospitalization and psychiatric treatment. The framework provided by nineteenth-century narratives offered no model for completely rejecting the existing models of psychiatric diagnosis and treatment. If a woman decided that she was mentally ill, the best that she could hope for was competent and compassionate care.

As Thomas Szasz has written, campaigning against the commitment of sane people is not enough. According to Szasz, "obsession with false commitment," which is the focus of many nineteenth-century madness narratives, "obscured the fundamental issue of freedom and responsibility of the so-called mad person, and reinforced the belief that incarcerating the truly insane was in the best interests of both the patient and society."[39] According to Szasz, the problem stems from psychiatric discourse itself. The question is not whether one is sane, but who determines sanity and insanity, and what happens to those deemed to be mentally ill. As Szasz writes, "Psychiatric diagnoses are stigmatizing labels, phrased to resemble medical diagnoses and applied to persons whose behavior annoys or offends others."[40] These labels are used to justify incarceration and other forms of forced treatment. Because Szasz believes that mental diseases are "invented" rather than "discovered,"[41] he insists that "There is no medical, moral, or legal justification for involuntary psychiatric interventions." According to Szasz, involuntary commitment and treatment are "crimes against humanity."[42] Furthermore, if, as Szasz believes, mental illness is a myth, then "there can be no hospitalization, treatment, or cure for it."[43] Psychiatric practice as we know it, then, is a sham at best and a crime at worst.

The reform efforts of the nineteenth-century did not go far enough for Szasz, but they were consistent with social theories of the time. Social reform movements relied on the belief in the capacity of society to solve its problems and the usefulness of institutions toward that end. Particularly during the Progressive Era, institutions were viewed as the way to eradicate many social ills. By the 1960s, however, many people viewed institutions with suspicion—if not outright contempt. As the 1960s generation "dropped out" of corporate America and "turned on" to psychedelic drugs, institutions and traditions were seen as weapons of social conformity that stifled individual freedom and interfered with personal growth. The counter-cultures of the 1960s rebelled against the "establishment" by rejecting the prescriptions and values of American society. Political movements pushed for more than reform; protests against U.S. involvement in Vietnam, campaigns to end racial and sexual discrimination, the rise of the black power movement and black nationalism, and the resurgence of feminism confronted traditional values and beliefs. Psychiatric practice also came under attack. The antipsychiatry movement developed within the profession of psychiatry, and antipsychiatry associations were also formed by patients themselves.

The 1960s also saw sweeping changes in the treatment of institutionalized mental patients. Antipsychotic medications had been developed in the 1950s, and miraculous cures were attributed to these drugs. Similar claims had been made about the effectiveness of shock therapies, but treatment with the new medications appeared to have more startling results. From the 1950s to the 1970s, countless mental patients were released from institutions, supposedly able to function in the community because of antipsychotic drugs. Instead of being housed in large institutions, these "outpatients" (later referred to as "clients" or, true to the capitalist spirit, "consumers") were to receive care and support from community mental health facilities. A new era in psychiatric treatment had begun.

Drawing on both historical and medical evidence, Andrew Scull rejects accounts that attribute deinstitutionalization to the "revolutionary" impact of psychoactive drugs. First of all, Scull shows that deinstitutionalization began in the late 1940s and early 1950s—*before* the new drugs were available.[44] His second objection is even more damaging to the "pharmacological explanation" for deinstitutionalization. As Scull points out, "a growing volume of evidence" suggests that the therapeutic effectiveness of psychoactive medications has been "greatly exaggerated."[45] According to Scull, deinstitutionalization determined how the new drugs would be used. Without the impetus provided by deinstitutionalization, psychoactive medications would have been used to manage patients within institutions rather than in community settings.[46]

Ideologically, there is nothing astounding about the use of drugs to manage—or control—the so-called mentally ill. "In the past, psychiatrists used their power to imprison individuals in mental hospitals for life," writes Szasz. "Now they use their power to drug patients for life."[47] Treatment with medication is entirely consistent with the medical model of mental illness. Just as drugs are used to alleviate physical conditions, antipsychotic medications were developed to treat severe mental illness. Drug therapies resulted from and subsequently reinforced biological psychiatry. As Russell writes,

> Biological psychiatry is the dominant form of psychology in the Western world. Its influence spreads far beyond actual treatment. It informs our ways of conceptualizing most forms of human distress and eccentricity. It is pervaded with an aura of certainty which makes challenges difficult.[48]

The apparent success of drug therapy supported the theory of biological bases for mental illness. If mental illness could be

treated by medication, then surely it was caused by an underlying biological disorder. "As the knowledge claims supporting
mainstream diagnostic systems become increasingly biomedi-
cal in nature," writes Laura Brown, "so too, do the diagnoses
themselves."[49]

In *They Say You're Crazy*, Paula Caplan examines the ideology of the American Psychiatric Association's *Diagnostic and
Statistical Manual of Mental Disorders*. According to Caplan,
the authors of the *DSM* wield tremendous power. "Decisions
about who is normal begin with at most a few dozen people—
mostly male, mostly white, mostly wealthy, mostly American
psychiatrists," she writes.[50] Caplan explains how, by following
the diagnostic criteria for Self-Defeating Personality Disorder
and Premenstrual Dysphoric Disorder, almost any woman
could be labeled "abnormal." If women are more likely to be
diagnosed with a psychiatric condition, then it follows that
they are also more vulnerable to psychiatric treatment, particularly drug therapies. Indeed, as Russell writes, "It is women
more than men who directly encounter biological psychiatry in
treatment."[51] While bearing in mind that there is no universal
patriarchy that oppresses women similarly regardless of context, it is important to note that psychiatry has a particular
function for women and other marginalized people. According
to Russell,

> The ideological factor which keeps biological psychiatry in posi-
> tion is that it is very good at doing what it was in fact set up to
> do, namely, to act as a moral guardian. Psychiatry turns women's
> discontent with patriarchy and protests against the social order
> into mental symptoms of underlying physical pathology. The inter-
> ests of patriarchy are then served very well.[52]

Feminism, the antipsychiatry movement, and other revolutionary philosophies had a significant impact on women's
madness narratives in the late twentieth century. Writers who
participated in antipsychiatry movements or were at least influenced by them were also more likely to resist the tendency
to internalize psychiatric oppression. Clearly, the return to
negative views of psychiatric treatment could be linked to several factors, including the publication of the critical works of
Laing, Szasz, and Foucault, the formation of advocacy groups

comprised of mental patients themselves, and the resurgence of the women's movement. Instead of providing sensational accounts of bizarre behavior and miraculous cures, Susanna Kaysen's *Girl, Interrupted*, Jill Johnston's *Paper Daughter*, and Kate Millett's *The Loony-Bin Trip* question modern psychiatric practice.

Susanna Kaysen's *Girl, Interrupted*, published in 1993, recounts her experiences of hospitalization in the late 1960s. Kaysen was admitted to McLean Hospital, a private institution in Boston, in 1967. Many of McLean's patients, including Kaysen, came from upper-class families. The hospital also has a history of caring for famous patients; Sylvia Plath, Robert Lowell, Ray Charles, and James Taylor were hospitalized at McLean. An expensive private hospital, McLean offered a much higher level of care than state institutions. In addition to having better facilities, McLean provided a better staff-patient ratio, and patients at McLean received more attention from doctors.

Despite the higher standards of care at McLean, *Girl, Interrupted* is reminiscent of nineteenth-century asylum autobiographies because of its critique of psychotherapy and inpatient psychiatric treatment. Like the accounts by Packard, Smith, and Lathrop, Kaysen's narrative depicts unsatisfactory grounds for her hospitalization. On her initial visit to a particular psychiatrist, the doctor asks her a few questions about pimples and boyfriends, and then decides she needs "a rest"—at McLean Hospital. "I'd never seen that doctor before," she writes, and "he decided to put me away after only fifteen minutes. . . . What about me was so deranged that in less than half an hour a doctor would pack me off to the nuthouse?"[53]

According to Kaysen, when people ask how she became a patient at McLean Hospital, "What they really want to know is if they are likely to end up in there as well"; her answer is, "It's easy":

And it is easy to slip into a parallel universe. There are so many of them: worlds of the insane, the criminal, the crippled, the dying, perhaps of the dead as well. These worlds exist alongside this world and resemble it, but are not in it.[54]

Although Kaysen is technically a voluntary patient, she doesn't choose to be hospitalized. "I signed myself in," she writes. "I had to, because I was of age. It was that or a court order, though they could never have gotten a court order against me. I didn't know that, so I signed myself in."[55] In addition, the doctor "tricks her" by telling her that she would be in the hospital for a couple of weeks. Kaysen was hospitalized for almost two years, and was granted her release when she became engaged. In effect, she is transferred from one male authority figure, the psychiatrist, to another, her fiancé.

Kaysen refers to her hospitalization as a "sentence" and describes her diagnosis as "the charges against me."[56] She notes that her diagnosis, borderline personality disorder, is more commonly diagnosed in women. Aware of gender biases in psychiatric diagnoses, Kaysen points out that "many disorders" are more commonly diagnosed in women. She uses "compulsive promiscuity" as an example. "How many girls do you think a seventeen-year-old boy would have to screw to earn the label 'compulsively promiscuous'?" she asks. "Probably in the fifteen-to-twenty range, would be my guess—if they ever put that label on boys, which I don't recall their doing."[57]

Clearly attuned to the ways gender influences psychiatric treatment, Kaysen describes a time she fell asleep during a session with her therapist:

> "You want to sleep with me," he crowed.
> I opened my eyes and looked at him. Sallow, bald early, and with pale pouches under his eyes, he wasn't anybody I wanted to sleep with.[58]

Kaysen's response to her analyst's interpretation reveals the sexual bias as well as the absurdity of his remark. Yet, the doctor has the power to make authoritative interpretations of patients' behaviors. In discussing the stigma of psychiatric diagnosis, Kaysen points out the power differential between doctor and patient. A psychiatrist who saw her after her discharge told her that "borderline personality" is "what they call people whose lifestyles bother them."[59] Kaysen agrees, but she recognizes the limits of her ability to question psychiatric diagnosis and practice. "He can say it because he's a doctor," observes Kaysen. "If I said it, nobody would believe me."[60]

Although her autobiography is not framed by expert commentary, she recognizes the power of psychiatric discourse to influence her readers. She continually tries to undercut psychiatric power by her observations and in the way she structures her narrative.

Kaysen employs several "postmodern" narrative techniques in *Girl, Interrupted*. The novel is a pastiche of sorts, containing Kaysen's personal narrative, various documents associated with her hospitalization and diagnosis, and stories about other patients. In a section entitled "Etiology," Kaysen lists several contradictory theories of mental illness without comment, and the implication is that, not only does she disagree with these explanations, but also that it does not matter which one is chosen:

This person is (pick one):
1) on a perilous journey from which we can learn much when he or she returns;
2) possessed by (pick one):
   a) the gods,
   b) God (that is, a prophet),
   c) Some bad spirits, demons, or devils,
   d) The Devil;
3) a witch;
4) bewitched (variant of 2);
5) bad, and must be isolated and punished;
6) ill, and must be isolated and treated by (pick one):
   a) purging and leeches,
   b) removing the uterus if the person has one,
   c) electric shock to the brain,
   d) cold sheets wrapped tight around the body,
   e) Thorazine or Stelazine;
7) ill, and must spend the next seven years talking about it;
8) a victim of society's low tolerance for deviant behavior;
9) sane in an insane world;
10) on a perilous journey from which he or she may never return.[61]

The most striking way in which Kaysen interrupts her narrative, however, is by directly addressing the reader. Knowing that her psychiatric history could cause people to discredit her narrative, Kaysen repeatedly challenges readers to accept her version of the story. One chapter is even entitled "Do You Believe Him or Me?" She is conscious of her audience, intentional about maintaining the integrity of her account, and insistent upon her authority as an autobiographer.

Kaysen comes to view hospitalization as a way of saying "no" to life. "My ambition was to negate," she writes. "The world, whether dense or hollow, provoked only my negations. . . . My hunger, my thirst, my loneliness and boredom and fear were all weapons aimed at my enemy, the world."[62] Her narrative depicts suffering inside and outside the mental hospital. The late sixties brought nightly news coverage of the Vietnam War, protests against racial discrimination, and student revolts.

> The world didn't stop because we weren't in it anymore, far from it. Night after night tiny bodies fell to the ground on our TV screen: black people, young people, Vietnamese people, poor people. . . .
>
> Then came the period when people we knew—not knew personally, but knew of—started falling to the ground: Martin Luther King, Robert Kennedy.[63]

In addition to the assassinations of famous leaders, friends and acquaintances were also dying. Kaysen tells of a friend whose body was found, partly decomposed, at the bottom of an elevator shaft. She also alludes to her own difficulties with relationships after her discharge from the hospital. *Girl, Interrupted* implicitly makes a point similar to *I Never Promised You a Rose Garden*. Both books indicate that even though people might be "cured" of mental illness, they are not protected from the injustices and tragedies of life. They can still suffer and die tragically, as does Dr. Fried's former patient, whose life ended at Dachau.

Suffering is an inescapable part of life; it is not confined to the "mad." The reality of suffering is an affront to those who would diagnose it, and the vicissitudes of human behavior contradict rigid distinctions between sanity and madness. "What would we be left with if we dropped the hard core of biological psychiatry?" asks Russell. "Instead of 'mad' experiences and behaviors crying out for explanation, we would have human experiences and behaviors."[64] There is no psychiatric treatment that will eliminate pain without destroying human experience. Kaysen's time in the parallel universe of the mental hospital was an interruption in the joys and sorrows of living "in the world."

Johnston and Millett were well known as writers and activists during Kaysen's hospitalization. In particular, they are strongly associated with the feminist and lesbian-feminist movements of the 1960s and 1970s, although both women have also been active in organizations opposed to forced hospitalization and treatment. Jill Johnston's *Paper Daughter*, which primarily relates the events of her life in the 1960s, is the second part of her autobiography. It was published in 1985, two years after the initial volume, *Mother Bound*.[65] Clearly informed by the antipsychiatry movement, *Paper Daughter* criticizes forced hospitalization and the institution of psychiatry.

The events of *Paper Daughter* occurred before Johnston wrote *Lesbian Nation* and even before she became a feminist. She writes that she was "unaffected by feminism" and, relatively late in the book, describes her first "glimpse" of feminist consciousness.[66] Diagnosed as "homosexual" (which was considered a disease at the time) and "schizophrenic," Johnston was hospitalized repeatedly. She calls herself "a child of the psychoanalytic age,"[67] and she often describes her thoughts and behavior in language derived from psychoanalytic frameworks. Although she criticizes psychiatry and psychiatric hospitalization, Johnston seems to accept some of the general insights of psychoanalytic theory.

Johnston does not comment explicitly about other women's autobiographies; however, she describes the internalized oppression evidenced in the majority of twentieth-century madness narratives. Her own writings on madness combine the rhetoric of the nineteenth century with the theories of Laing and Szasz. She calls madness a "thought crime" and a criminal act "subject to that arm of the penal system called Institutional Psychiatry."[68] Johnston's critique focuses particularly on the treatment of women; she associates psychiatric imprisonment with the Inquisition (as Packard and Szasz had done before her). As Johnston writes, "The law enforcement agency of the Inquisition in its older form of the Church and its new form of the Modern Psychiatric Profession is primarily an agency to keep women in their place and exterminate them if they can't."[69]

Johnston refuses to give ultimate authority to the so-called experts and says, "I want to know when I get to be my own authority."[70] In an article written before *Paper Daughter*, Johnston describes the "internalized Other" (a term from object relations theory) of the psychiatric patient:

> It isn't just the world out there that's reluctant to grant any person their own authority, it's the world inside yourself and a part of that world for me is the internalized Inquisitor of the hospital system who indicated by the most elaborate punitive modern machinery that if I thought I wasn't much of anybody *before* my "experience" I could be certain that what I had become was a total non person in a non environment of my own non making.[71]

Agreeing with Szasz that psychiatric hospitalization is a form of social control, Johnston quotes from his writings at length more than once in *Paper Daughter*. Echoing Szasz, she writes,

> the psychiatric hospital is still, after several centuries, a catch-all for various sorts of misfits: the dispossessed, the unemployed, the ill or hungry, the self-abused, the suicidal or depressed, the immoral, the criminal, the homosexual, the eccentric and the foolish—as well as the genuinely demented, *if there is such a thing.*[72]

Johnston does more than classify psychiatric patients as misfits, and her account of the patient population at Bellevue is consistent with Peter Breggin's observation that

> The main characteristics of state mental hospital inmates . . . are poverty, homelessness, and lack of family or community support. Surely, many psychiatric inmates seem grossly irrational—but many do not. And irrational or not, they end up in the hospital for reasons other than their mental condition. Powerlessness is the key to becoming a psychiatric inmate.[73]

Paper Daughter both explicates and illustrates the powerlessness of psychiatric inmates.

Although Johnston criticizes the "treatment" of institutionalized mental patients, she reserves her sharpest criticisms for the institution of psychiatry. Her analyses of madness and psychiatric power are consistent with the main currents of antipsychiatry, particularly Laing's early work. Clearly influenced by Laing's perspective, Johnston questions the notion of equating "the crazy trip," as she refers to her experience, with "mental illness." After her hospitalizations, she "[became] convinced that the best place to be was crazy, if only I could find out how to stay clear of America's loony bins."[74] Johnston defends Laing's approach by maintaining that neither she nor Laing has romanticized madness.

Laing has been frequently criticized for romanticizing madness. As Ussher points out, antipsychiatry has been ridiculed for the notion that madness is related to thwarted creativity; "the mad in the back wards are clearly revealed not to be tortured artists," she writes.[75] Showalter has criticized antipsychiatry on the basis of sexual bias. For all the "feminist" promise of Laing's theories, she writes, "antipsychiatry had no coherent analysis to offer to women."[76] Moreover, Showalter describes unethical forms of treatment. According to Showalter, David Cooper "advocates sex with patients, which he calls 'bed therapy,' as a useful way to establish contact." With the practice of sexual exploitation, "the promises of antipsychiatry for women are fully betrayed, and we seem to have returned to a Victorian saga of the wrongs of women comparable to the rape of asylum patients by their keepers."[77] Yet, other women have rejected antipsychiatry outright. For instance, Brown writes that it is neither "clinically [nor] politically useful to glamorize distress, as did R. D. Laing and other psychiatric radicals, as 'madness' to be savored and entered fully into."[78]

However, Johnston's critique (and, in all fairness, Laing's as well) goes beyond a romanticizing of madness. She insists that "mental illness" should not be treated as a medical disease and therefore objects to drug therapy. According to Johnston, psychiatric medications "disorient and incapacitate" people; she describes herself as having walked around in a "Thorazine trance."[79] "I was led to believe that Thorazine probably saved my life," she writes. "Later I became even more convinced that a life saved by Thorazine in a mental hospital was not particularly worth living."[80] She equates giving someone a psychiatric diagnosis with name-calling and emphasizes the dehumanizing elements of hospitalization. "After a bath and a change of clothes to hospital gear," she writes, "I was officially a paper daughter, one who exists only on paper, a name and a diagnosis."[81] The significance of her experiences of hospitalization, diagnosis, and treatment is apparent by the decision to title the book *Paper Daughter*.

Since the publication of *Paper Daughter*, Johnston has not published any other autobiographical volumes. Part of the reason may be that *Mother Bound* and *Paper Daughter* are fairly traditional autobiographies. In a talk given in 1994 and later published, Johnston rejects traditional autobiographical form in favor of what she refers to as the new women's autobiography. "In the traditional autobiography, the male form, the life is lived first, then written," Johnston maintains. "The genre has been in effect an award form, a vehicle to celebrate achievement." According to Johnston, "The subject of the traditional autobiography is what is over, done, a record of fulfillment—the fulfillment of the promise of privileges that had been *given*."[82]

On the other hand, Johnston considers "the invention of the self or self as subject" as the central concept in the new women's autobiography.[83] "Writing and self-creation are synonymous," Johnston claims. "[T]he life that was *given*, our inglorious past, is no longer what is written or written about"; moreover, "Nothing is written *about* at all."[84] According to Johnston, "When [lesbians] write the life we are making it up—not the facts, oh we cherish the facts, but the ways of seeing and organizing them—and this is a political act of self-recognition."[85] Although Johnston emphasizes the particular role of lesbians in rewriting the past, the same can be said of women mental patients, who have often been silenced or disregarded. Madness narratives allow women to describe and interpret their own experiences.

Kate Millett has also articulated and practiced a new way of life writing. Instead of Johnston's "write first, then live," Millett's approach could be described as writing *and* living. Millett is truly practicing life writing. In *Flying*, she writes, "*it had occurred to me to treat my own existence as documentary*," and she decides to treat herself as "subject matter."[86] Her autobiographical method is taken from filmmaking techniques, and she describes her method as "Taking wing into a scatter shot of movie notions, ways to capture the living present. Preserve the life we know, reinterpret, present in our terms as women."[87] She practices this approach in her autobiographical writings, which include *Flying*, *Sita*,[88] and *The Loony-Bin Trip*.

Autobiography, however, can be risky, and Millett discusses the possibility of turning her work into fiction, "out of the suspect waters of the personal, the autobiographical, the experiential" and into the "safe harbor of fiction."[89] Despite the vulnerability of treating her life as subject matter, Millett decides that it is necessary. In a conversation with Doris Lessing, Millett says that she is "always embarrassed."

> "Have so much to be self-conscious about. Doing it in the first person which seems necessary somehow, much of the point is lost in my case if I didn't put myself on the line. But feeling so vulnerable, my god, a Lesbian. Sure, an experience of human beings. But not described. Not permitted. It has no traditions. No language. No history of agreed values."[90]

Autobiographical writing enables Millett to name her experiences of loving women and of madness in a manner that cannot be accomplished in fiction. The disguises of fiction perpetuate silences. As Adrienne Rich has written,

> Whatever is unnamed, undepicted in images, whatever is omitted from biography, censored in collections of letters, whatever is misnamed as something else, made difficult-to-come-by, whatever is buried in the memory by the collapse of meaning under an inadequate or lying language—this will become, not merely unspoken, but *unspeakable*.[91]

In addition to articulating her experiences, Millett wishes to challenge the traditional separation of the public and personal. "In discovering the vital integrity of all human experience," she says at a feminist rally, "we've reintegrated and subsumed these artificial distinctions."[92]

Instead of asserting, as Johnston does, that writing and self-creation are the same thing, Millett ponders whether the act of writing changes experiences. "Does consciousness of an experience change it?" she asks.

> Does the selection of a day—that you begin by knowing you must remember and observe—really affect it? Do you change the balance, distort the truth? The period itself, its choice and selection,

does that not in itself constitute a kind of misconstruction, and the rest follow subconsciously? . . . What do you leave out, what do you falsify? What do you mar by the imposition of a pattern?[93]

Even if Millett could use writing like a camera to record her experiences, there is still an editing process. Referring perhaps to an early draft of *The Loony-Bin Trip*, she writes,

I should be writing Chapter One today. Just beginning to take shape, how to do it. Going back to when I was crazy and unable to start. Frightens me to go back there, afraid I'll go crazy again putting myself in that pit as I have to just to write it.[94]

Millett seems intent to recreate the experience, but she also wants to explain it to herself.[95] The act of writing is also an act of interpretation.

The Loony-Bin Trip, Millett's account of coercive treatment and forced hospitalization, offers a powerful critique of commitment procedures and psychiatric practice. *The Loony-Bin Trip*, which was published in 1994, has very few elements of sensational accounts of madness and forced treatment; instead, it moves into the realm of social theory. In Millett's narrative, not only does the personal become the political, but also the theoretical is primarily based on lived experience. Unlike some twentieth-century narratives of mental illness, Millett offers a straightforward account of her experiences and makes no attempt to hide her personal history. By telling of her own experiences of "mental illness" and forced hospitalization, Millett advocates new ways of thinking about the mind and its capacities.

It is clear from the opening pages of the book that Millett will tell her story in her own terms. *The Loony-Bin Trip* begins with an exuberant description of sexual intimacy between Millett and her lover, Sophie. The opening serves to establish Millett's world as lesbian or woman-identified. Such a world represents a revolutionary way of living in a patriarchal society. In addition, the sexually explicit opening of *The Loony-Bin Trip* also positions the reader as a voyeur. The construction of the reader as voyeur is significant in a madness narrative. In an era in which personal accounts of mental illness become national bestsellers, a substantial portion of the audience for these books probably reads them from a voyeuristic perspective. The reading experience is akin to peeping into the lives of the mentally ill and vicariously experiencing the "sordid" world of madness.

In *Flying*, Millett associates societal disapproval of lesbianism with the social stigma of madness. Both are taboo subjects, and society expects lesbians and mad women to be silent and remain out of sight. Millett writes about hiding her craziness "so that I do not shock or give offense, foreseeing that the sight would be obscene, upsetting."[96] Remembering a time that her mother asked if she were in love with another women, Millett writes, "The accusation convicted me already of madness, obscenity, the unspeakable."[97] According to Millett,

> Homosexuality was invented by a straight world dealing with its own bisexuality. But finding this difficult, and preferring not to admit it, it invented a pariah state, a leper colony for the incorrigible whose very existence, when tolerated openly, was admonition to all. We queers keep everyone straight as whores keep matrons virtuous.[98]

Similarly, in *The Loony-Bin Trip* she would come to understand madness as an invention to enforce social conformity. Millett's autobiographies counter these attitudes by giving voice to her experiences without apology; lesbianism and madness are transformed from the unspeakable to the spoken, and lesbian sexuality is celebrated and not condemned.

The initial exuberance of *The Loony-Bin Trip* does not last long. Soon, Sophie and the women interns at Millett's farm are chastising her for discontinuing her medication. Almost everything she does is seen as an indication of mental illness. Eventually, Millett's family and friends attempt to force her into treatment, which forces Millett to fight for her freedom. Everyone involved appears to be convinced that he or she is acting on Millett's behalf, even though very few people are willing to listen to her perspective.

Although she avoids commitment in the United States, she is hospitalized involuntarily in Ireland. Released through the help of friends, Millett returns to New York and seeks treatment for manic-depression. "Defeated" after her experiences in Ireland, Millett acquiesces to the perspective she tried to

fight on the farm. When the women on Millett's farm were convinced that she had an illness that must be treated with medication, Millett resisted. After her experience in Ireland,
however, Millett makes an appointment with a psychiatrist so
that she can get a prescription for lithium. "You must say you
are crazy," she tells herself,

> say it, kiss the rod. Unless you repent to this stuffed shirt there is
> no lithium pill, no chemical cure, the precious prophylactic against
> your ups and downs, the vicious cycle of manic episode and depres-
> sion. It balances and prevents, keeps you on an even keel. . . . Life
> under lithium; a peculiar, submerged, slightly sedated, and ever so
> slightly depressed life. Slow—but passably normal.[99]

Millett "confesses" to be crazy, and gets a prescription for lithium and another appointment with the psychiatrist. Although
her treatment is voluntary, she views it as submission.

Most of *The Loony-Bin Trip* emphasizes the right of individuals to choose whether to receive psychiatric treatment; however, Millett finally ends up questioning the whole system of
psychopathology. Millett describes periods in which she saw a
psychiatrist regularly and dutifully took her medication. She
also recounts times that she argued against involuntary hospitalization by claiming that she was not mentally ill. But Millett's documentary style allows readers to follow the change in
her thinking. Although she argues that she is sane earlier in the
book, by the end she rejects the entire model of mental illness.
When she begins to reach this point she thinks to herself and,
through the use of second-person pronouns, tells her readers:

> you will have to stop equating madness with captivity; that is stop
> proving you aren't crazy, since this assumes that if you were, you
> might deserve to be locked up: you're only innocent if you're sane,
> and so on.[100]

According to Millett, the most effective way to fight involuntary hospitalization is to accept madness while simultaneously
rejecting the need for psychiatric treatment. "Not till you permit madness," she tells herself, "can you really stand against
the bin as prison and punishment."[101] She stops going to the
psychiatric clinic, discontinues her medication, and eventually
becomes part of the antipsychiatry movement.

Like Johnston, Millett is influenced by the work of Laing and Szasz, and she also rejects prevailing notions of psychopathology and the need to "treat" or control those diagnosed as mentally ill. Millett argues against attempts to confine and control madness. "If we go mad—so what?" she asks. "We would come back again if not chased away, exiled, isolated, confined."[102] *The Loony-Bin Trip* implicitly questions the approach of reformers who maintain the bifurcation of sanity and madness. Clearly, she agrees with Szasz's assertion that the focus on false commitment obscures the problems with contemporary psychiatric practice. The overarching problem is the ideology of mental illness, which allows psychiatrists to label some people as mentally ill and then treat them for their own good or for the protection of society. "Say that you were mad," writes Millett of her hospitalization in Ireland,

> they still have no right to put you here [in a mental institution], deprive you of your liberty and even hope. Laing believes that and Szasz and David Cooper . . . . No one else believes it at all. That, finally, is the problem.[103]

Millett, then, does not advocate mere reform of psychiatric treatment or commitment laws, although she does call for an end to forced hospitalization, drugging, electroshock, and "definitions of insanity as a crime to be treated with savage methods."[104] Like Foucault and Szasz, she sees psychiatric hospitalization as a form of social control. "[T]he madhouse lives for us all," she writes.

> This is the jail we could all end up in. And we know it. And watch our step. For a lifetime. We behave. A fantastic and entire system of social control, by the threat of example as effective over the general population as detention centers in dictatorships, the image of the madhouse floats through every mind for the course of its lifetime. . . . surely it is the law of Thought Crime to forbid, punish, or incarcerate different thoughts. Mental activity at the margin. Or over the line.[105]

Ultimately, Millett questions the whole concept of "mental illness" and the psychiatric basis for imposing psychiatric diagnoses.

Even though the madness narratives of Packard, Smith, and

Lathrop discuss such issues as psychiatric power and the particular vulnerability of women, they focus primarily on the incarceration of sane persons. Ironically, this reinforcement of the sane/insane binarism set the stage for women to accept the psychopathologizing tendencies of the twentieth century. Kaysen, Johnston, and Millett, on the other hand, resist internalized oppression and question psychiatric diagnoses, particularly the classification of women as either sane or insane. *The Loony-Bin Trip* goes beyond the madness narratives of the nineteenth century in that it calls for revolution rather than reform. With Millett's autobiography, madness narratives branch out in new directions. *The Loony-Bin Trip* indicates the continuing relevance of madness narratives to discussions of psychiatric practice, individual freedom, and social justice.

5

Seasons of Peril: The Madness Narratives of Janet Frame and Bessie Head

MADNESS NARRATIVES BY AMERICAN WOMEN TRADITIONALLY stress content and message over the form of the narrative; however, Mary Jane Ward, Susanna Kaysen, Jill Johnston, and Kate Millett pay particular attention to the craft of writing and the construction of their narratives. Unlike many of the writers of earlier madness narratives, Ward, Kaysen, Johnston, and Millett are concerned with form as well as content. In general, autobiographical accounts of madness from the latter part of the twentieth century, particularly those that are critical of psychiatric practices, tend to pay more attention to the form of the narrative.

New Zealand writer Janet Frame and African writer Bessie Head have taken the art of the madness narrative even further than American women writers. Frame's *Faces in the Water* and Head's *A Question of Power* combine form and content in ways that fully utilize the potential of the novel as a medium for madness narratives. Like other late-twentieth-century madness narratives, the autobiographical writings of Frame and Head articulate the fundamental questions of power that must be asked about ideologies of madness. In their novels, however, the union of aesthetics and politics surpasses that of previous madness narratives. Frame and Head are concerned with significant issues other than madness and, in addition, use their madness narratives to address intersecting questions of power. The thematic layering of *Faces in the Water* and *A Question of Power* implies that various questions of power are interrelated and, moreover, that the rhetoric of mental illness functions similarly to other oppressive discourses.

In *Faces in the Water*, which was first published in 1961,

111

Frame describes many of her own experiences through the first-person narrative of Istina Mavet. Yet, she also distances herself from her protagonist, insisting that Istina is not a self-portrait. As Frame writes in her autobiography,

> In my book *Faces in the Water* I have described in detail the surroundings and events in the several mental hospitals I experienced during the eight following years [after 1945]. . . . The fiction of the book lies in the portrayal of the central character, based on my life but given largely fictional thoughts and feelings, to create a picture of the sickness I saw around me.[1]

According to Vanessa Finney, "It is Istina Mavet who controls the narratives of the years Frame spent in hospital; Frame's own point of view is not recorded, except from the distance of the narrator of the autobiography."[2] Many critics, including Finney, have seen *Faces in the Water* as a fictitious representation of Frame's years in mental hospitals. According to Suzette Henke, "The odd thing about Frame's descriptions of mental illness is the lacuna in her narrative when she attempts to depict life in a mental institution."[3]

Just as Frame has denied any association, other than experiential, between herself and Istina, some critics decided almost immediately that such a correlation was impossible. In her autobiography, Frame refers to a reviewer's remark that " 'the use of the first person was a mistake. A woman who has been what this woman has been would never be able to remember and write about it in this way.' "[4] Simon Petch speculates that Frame's amusement at the reviewer's remark "must have masked anxiety, for originally Istina Mavet had been safely killed off to sever any autobiographical connection." He points out that an unpublished version of *Faces in the Water* included a postscript to indicate that Istina Mavet eventually committed suicide. According to Petch,

> [Frame's] decision to keep the ending open by leaving Istina alive also keeps open, however cautiously, the life-lines between autobiography and fiction, and between Janet Frame and the narrator she has created to displace and resurrect herself.[5]

One of Frame's reasons for writing her autobiography was to correct the image of her that had been created in part by *Faces in the Water. "Faces in the Water* was autobiographical in the sense that everything happened, but the central character was invented," Frame has stated. She turned from fiction to autobiography because "I wanted to write my story, and . . . to correct some things which have been taken as fact and are not fact. My fiction is genuinely fiction. And I do invent things." Frame has also stated that she is "always in fictional mode."[6] "I look at everything from the point of view of fiction," she said in an interview with Elizabeth Alley, "and so it wasn't a change to be writing autobiography except that autobiography was more restrictive because it was based in fact, and I wanted to make an honest record of my life." She describes autobiography as "found fiction"; "I was still bound by the choice of words and the shaping of the book, and that is similar to when one is writing fiction."[7]

Frame was a patient in New Zealand mental hospitals during the forties and fifties; therefore, *Faces in the Water* portrays the same era of psychiatric hospitalization as *The Snake Pit* and *I Never Promised You a Rose Garden*. Although there are many parallels between *Faces in the Water* and *The Snake Pit,* Frame's novel departs significantly from the earlier work by Ward. The similarities between *Faces in the Water* and *I Never Promised You a Rose Garden* are largely confined to the descriptions of the living conditions at the hospitals. The beginning of *Faces in the Water* inverts the message of *I Never Promised You a Rose Garden* about the impossibility of protecting people from the world outside the hospital. The hospital is a dangerous place for Istina, the protagonist of *Faces in the Water*. As the novel opens, we do not know anything about the narrator or the setting. The narrative opens with an odd invocation to "Safety," which precedes the description of the time that Istina will call "the season of peril."[8]

They have said that we owe allegiance to Safety, that he is our Red Cross who will provide us with ointment and bandages for our wounds and remove the foreign ideas the glass beads of fantasy the bent hairpins of unreason embedded in our minds. On all the doors which lead to and from the world they have posted warning notices and lists of safety measures to be taken in extreme emergency. . . . how can we find our path in sleep and dreams and preserve ourselves from their dangerous reality of lightening snakes traffic

germs riot earthquakes blizzard and dirt when lice creep like rid-
dles through our minds? Quick, where is the Red Cross God with
the ointment and plaster the needle and thread the clean linen
bandages to mummify our festering dreams? Safety first.[9]

Faces in the Water is the story of Istina's struggle to safeguard
her passions, her "glass beads of fantasy," and her very self
from the "dangerous reality" of psychiatric practice.

The narrative of *Faces in the Water*, unlike the opening of
The Snake Pit, quickly clarifies the setting and the perspective.
After a brief opening section, which introduces the issues of
safety and danger, and reality and fantasy, Istina explicitly
states the subject of the story. "I will write about the season of
peril," she says. "I was put in hospital because a great gap
opened in the ice floe between myself and the other people
whom I watched with their world, drifting away . . . I was alone
on the ice."[10] Although cut off from others, Istina's narrative
often uses collective pronouns such as "we" and "us" as well
as "they" and "them." In this way she subtly draws readers
onto the ice and into the danger, just as the narrative techniques of *The Snake Pit* encourage readers to identify with
Virginia Cunningham.

Despite the difference in cultural context, Frame's descriptions of the conditions at the hospitals match many of the characteristics of Juniper Hill, the fictional hospital in *The Snake
Pit*. Istina, like Virginia, is transferred at will from ward to
ward and subject not only to the daily schedule but also to un-
expected deviations from it. Frame and Ward use the same
joke to indicate the impersonal way the patients are prodded
through the daily routine. Istina and Virginia turn such orders
as "Cafeteria, Ladies" into an anonymous mass of "Cafeteria
Ladies." Meals at Treecroft have the same frantic pace of those
at Juniper Hill, and the dining room is quickly vacated. "There
seemed a haste, an urgency about everything," Istina tells us.
"[T]ea was quickly finished and the knives counted, and there
was a feeling in the air that the most important events of the
day were about to occur."[11] In general, though, the sense of
time is completely distorted. As Istina tells us, "There is no
past present or future" in the mental hospital.[12]

Constant surveillance adds another element of unreality to
the world of the hospital. Privacy is rare in most of the wards

where Istina is a patient. The bathroom stalls do not have doors, and the nurses observe the patients while they are on the toilets. During Istina's confinement at Cliffhaven, she refuses to use the toilet while the nurse is watching; "the nurse pulled down my pants and forced me onto the seat," she writes.[13] At Treecroft she is sometimes prohibited from going to the bathroom when she needs to. "I would slide from my seat under the table and wet on the floor like an animal."[14] Washing and dressing are also dehumanizing experiences at Treecroft. Istina describes how the patients at Treecroft were "crowded" into the washroom to be dressed. "There was little hope of washing," she says. "We stood there naked, packed tightly like cattle at the saleyards, and awaiting the random distribution of our clothes which usually arrived with one or two articles missing."[15] When Istina finds herself without pants, she complains to the nurse, who tells her that she has no need of pants. In addition to being without pants and stockings on occasion, Istina was also denied sanitary napkins. "I dreaded every month when I would have to ask for sanitary napkins which were supplied by the hospital," she says, "for once or twice I was refused them, and told by the overworked besieged staff, 'Use your arse hole.' "[16]

Some of the hospitals described in *Faces in the Water* practice "modern treatment." Istina's characterizations of "modern" attitudes toward "mental illness" are clearly ironic. The "new" attitude, according to Istina, is that "mental patients are like you and me." The new attitude, she says, "seemed to predominate the bright counterpanes, pastel-shaded walls supposed to soothe, a few abstract paintings hanging paint-in-cheek in the sitting room; tables for four in the dining room, gay with checked cloths." However, it is all a disguise "to keep the pretense that Treecroft was a hotel, not a mental hospital, and anyway the words *mental hospital* were now frowned upon; the proper designation was now *psychiatric unit*."[17] Despite the appearance of Ward Seven, the ratio of patients to doctors is still extraordinarily inadequate. At Treecroft, one doctor is responsible for a thousand patients. As Susan Schwartz writes, "The 'new attitude' must be understood more in terms of society wishing to see itself as humane, than as a significant shift in the understanding of madness."[18]

Patients contribute to the pretense even after they are discharged. Istina reports that patients from Treecroft's Ward Seven went home promising "to spread the news that mental hospitals were certainly not what people seemed to think, that the letters full of shocking details that appeared in the newspapers were the work of cranks and liars." Indeed, "had not the patients of Ward Seven seen for themselves the modern conditions?" she asks, "that patients were regarded as human beings and cared for with kindness?" Istina quickly adds an understated and ironic comment about electroshock therapy: "Certainly shock treatment was unpleasant but after all it was for people's own good wasn't it; besides, it was held in another ward, and you were so dopey going and coming that you didn't remember much anyway."[19] The hospital staff justifies the new treatments as being for the good of the patients. According to Istina, " 'For your own good' is a persuasive argument that will eventually make man agree to his own destruction."[20]

Istina not only portrays the dehumanizing routines of mental hospitals, but also describes numerous instances of the staff's abusive treatment of patients. The patients are provoked into fighting for the amusement of the staff, and some patients are baited so that the staff can administer various punishments. At these moments, "the tension which mounted and reached its peak at intervals—both in the patients and in the nurses . . . —found its release, for a time."[21] Istina is "filled with disgust that the staff had so far forgotten that the people in their charge were human beings, as to treat them like animals in a pen at the zoo." Yet, Istina also recognizes that the hospital system has contributed to the nurses' behavior. She says that they "had long ago had to suppress any desire to 'nurse' and were now overworked, degraded, in many cases sadistic, custodians."[22] Although she does not excuse their behavior, she understands that the nurses' dehumanizing treatment of patients reflects their own lack of human dignity. Despite attempts to see patients as people like themselves, the separation between patients and staff—and even different levels of patients and staff—is firmly maintained. At Cliffhaven, even the staff coffee cups are marked and kept separate from the ones used by patients.

According to Istina, the nurses are to be feared because of their power to influence the course of treatment. They can get patients put on the list for shock treatments and sometimes on the lobotomy list as well. One of the main terrors in *Faces in the Water*, as in *The Snake Pit*, is the threat of electroshock therapy; according to Istina, "the fear leads in some patients to more madness." Through Istina's narrative, Frame associates shock treatments (EST) with electrocution, an analogy that had been used by Ward and would later be implied by Sylvia Plath (in *The Bell Jar*). "We know the rumors attached to E.S.T.," Istina tells us; "it is training for Sing Sing when we are at last convicted of murder and sentenced to death and sit strapped in the electric chair with the electrodes touching our skin through slits in our clothing."[23]

Unlike Virginia Cunningham and Esther Greenwood (the protagonists of Ward's and Plath's novels), Istina Mavet unequivocally presents electroshock as punishment for misbehavior. Istina characterizes shock treatment as "the new and fashionable means of quieting people and of making them realize that orders are to be obeyed."[24] Istina describes a time that she heard "sinister whispering" in the hallway outside her door:

> I had been unusually difficult that day in obeying orders, had "talked back" to the nurses, had screamed out of hopelessness; and now I was apprehensive, wondering what my punishment would be. The voices continued their whispering.
> "We'll give her shock treatment tomorrow," one said. "A worse shock than she's ever had. . . ."
> "Yes," replied the other, "She's down for shock. It will put her in her place I tell you. She needs to be taught a lesson. . . ."[25]

Faces in the Water never intimates that shock treatment might have therapeutic value. Instead, Istina portrays EST as a very effective tool of domination and a punishment for recalcitrant patients.

Although the mental hospital proves to be dangerous territory, Istina finds a certain degree of safety in her confinement. She sees this security in other patients, and it disturbs her. When she describes the hurried meals at Treecroft, Istina refers to the patients as "automatons":

> they were automatons geared to a pitch of excitement they could not understand and fearful lest whatever or whoever controlled them should tire of giving them distraction, and let them run down

like broken toys and have to find in their own selves a way of overcoming the desolation in which they lived.[26]

The world outside is also perilous, and many of the patients are
afraid of leaving the hospital. Istina shares this fear, but she is
more afraid of being alienated from herself. She is frightened
of the way Mrs. Pilling, a patient at Cliffhaven, accepts her life
there. "She seems like someone who could set up camp in a
graveyard and continue to boil the billy, eat and sleep soundly
and perhaps spend the day polishing tombstones or weeding
the graves," Istina tells us. "One watches her for a ripple of
herself as one watches an eternally calm lake for evidence of
the rumored creature inhabiting perhaps 'deeper than ever
plummet sounded.' One needs a machine like a bathysphere to
find Mrs. Pilling."[27]

For Istina, then, the choice is not between safety and danger,
but between the perils of her passion and the perils of their
alienation. In the extended analogy that compares electroshock and electrocution, Istina presents an unforgettable
image that can also be interpreted as an image of people being
consumed by their own passion. "[O]ur hair is singed as we
die," Istina says, "and the last smell in our nostrils is the smell
of ourselves burning."[28] She repeatedly refers to the danger of
losing herself and the threat of thieves who would steal parts
of her identity. As a whole, her experience of institutionalization involves both loss of self and the impositions of doctors
and hospital staff. "I did not know my identity," she says; "I
was burgled of body and hung in the sky like a woman of
straw."[29]

After several years of hospitalization, Istina learns through
a nurse's "hints" that, in Istina's words: "it was impossible for
me to continue living as myself, that I must be changed."[30] The
method of change is lobotomy, and Istina's mother consents to
the operation. According to Istina, the nurses had decided that
she had not learned her lesson and, having failed to "force it
upon [her]," had advised a " 'change of personality.' "[31] Similarly, the doctor tells her, " 'You will be changed. . . . The tension will be reduced.' "[32] However, Istina understands
lobotomy as an assault or demolition of the self:

with the doctors' advice and approval and my parents' consent, the
self that for nearly thirty years had fought with time and, pain-

stakingly, like a colony of ants bearing away the slain army, had carried the dead seconds, minutes, hours, over the difficult, slowly habitual tracks to the nest, the central storehouse—that self was to be assaulted, perhaps demolished.[33]

"I will be 'retrained'—that is the word used for lobotomy cases," Istina says. "Fitted, my mind cut and tailored to the ways of the world."[34]

The impending operation occupies Istina's thoughts constantly:

> The thought of the operation became a nightmare. Every morning when I woke I imagined, Today they will seize me, shave my head, dope me, send me to the hospital in the city, and when I open my eyes I will have a bandage over my head and a scar at each temple or a curved one, like a halo, across the top of my head where the thieves, wearing gloves and with permission and delicacy, have entered and politely ransacked the storehouse and departed calm and unembarrassed like meter readers, furniture removers, or decorators sent to repaper an upstairs room.[35]

The juxtaposition of "seize" and "thieves" with "permission" and "delicacy" exposes the incongruity of the action, in which the surgeon-thief has permission to "politely ransack" her brain with the nonchalance of a meter reader. The scar, perhaps resembling a halo, indicates that the "upstairs room" has been redecorated, the self remodeled so that it fits in better with the world.

Istina escapes the lobotomy by means of what appears to be a doctor's random decision. As the doctor is walking through the ward one day, Istina asks him what he thinks about the operation. "Patients did not usually interrupt his rounds," Istina says, "and any delay in his progress caused as much concern among the staff as if an important train carrying bullion had been held up by bandits."[36] Because she asks a vague question, " 'What is your opinion?' " the doctor does not know at first what she is talking about. Once he realizes what she is asking, he "instantly" says "no" to the lobotomy. " 'I don't want you changed,' " he replies. " 'I want you to stay as you are.' "[37]

Before her "reprieve," Istina wages a desperate battle to retain her sense of self. Confined to a seclusion room, she takes a pencil, which a sympathetic nurse had sneaked into the room along with a magazine, and writes all the verses she can re-member. "With the pencil I wrote on the wall snatches of re-membered poems but the pencil applied to the Brick Building wall was like a revolutionary dye that refuses to 'take,' " she says; "the two elements were antagonistic and the words suf-fered the cruelty of indistinctness or, out of self-defense, they preferred to remain aloof, unformed." The head nurse makes Istina wash the writing off the wall, but the poems continue to sustain her. "I recited poems to myself or sang or, silent, re-membered and feared."[38] Terrified of losing her sense of self, Istina focuses on the things that determine her identity: poetry, songs, and memories.

In Frame's narratives, writing and re-membering the self are shown to be essential for survival. Unlike autobiographers who write to give others hope in the power of doctors to cure mental illness, Frame writes for the women she met in institutions. "It was their sadness and courage and my desire to 'speak' for them that enabled me to survive," she writes.[39] In part, Frame writes to ensure that these women do not become forgotten "faces in the water." In *Faces in the Water*, Istina describes how she feels while she listens to another patient play the piano:

> Listening to her, one experienced a deep uneasiness as of having avoided an urgent responsibility, like someone who, walking at night along the banks of a stream, catches a glimpse in the water of a white face or a moving limb and turns quickly away, refusing to help or to search for help.

According to Istina, "We all see faces in the water":

> We smother our memory of them, even our belief in their reality, and become calm people of the world; or we can neither forget nor help them. Sometimes by a trick of circumstances or dream or a hostile neighborhood of light we see our own face.[40]

The image of faces in the water—faces that might be our own—links people in and out of the hospital much better than the "mental patients are just like us" attitude. In addition, *Faces in the Water* suggests that mental patients might be dif-ferent from other people, at least in the way they view the world. As Istina says, "I knew the mad language which created with words, without using reason, has a new shape of reason; as the blind fashion from touch an effective shape of the sight denied them." Moreover, she also knows "that the people about me dared to believe what few others are even half afraid to suspect; that things are not what they seem."[41] According to Schwartz, "The madwoman [in Frame's fiction] is representative of the ontological fragmentation that the sane, in misrecognizing themselves as whole, refuse to see."[42]

Istina rejects the romantic notion that madness is akin to genius. "There is an aspect of madness which is seldom mentioned in fiction because it would damage the romantic popular idea of the insane as a person whose speech appeals as immediately poetic," she tells us. "Few of the people who roamed the dayroom would have qualified as acceptable heroines, in popular taste; few were charmingly uninhibited eccentrics."[43] Although *Faces in the Water* neither romanticizes madness nor characterizes the mad as frustrated artists, it implies that the mad can see beyond consensual reality. Therefore, the sickness Istina observes around her cannot simply be equated with "mental illness." The sickness is also not limited to the patients; it is shared by the hospital staff and the world outside. Istina says that separating the staff cups from those of the patients "prevent[s] the interchange of diseases like boredom loneliness authoritarianism."[44] Nurses show themselves to be sick by their inhuman treatment of patients, and by their behavior the nurses' humanity is distorted or "diseased." As Paulo Freire writes, "Dehumanization marks not only those whose humanity has been stolen, but also (though in a different way) those who have stolen it." According to Freire, dehumanization is "a *distortion* of the vocation of becoming more fully human."[45]

Society shows its sickness by forcing people to conform, and doctors carry out the dicta of society through confinement, treatment and, in the case of psychosurgery, cutting people to make a better "fit" with the world. The patients, on the other hand, are "caged within [themselves],"[46] fearful of the dangers and longing for some security. In such a devil's bargain, the perils to the individual include loss of self and total surrender to the dangers (or the safety) of either the hospital or the outside world. The perils to society include the loss of human potential, the creation of automatons, and the destruction of society that ensues when dehumanizing treatment is not only deemed acceptable but also seen as necessary.

The impact of authoritarianism and forced conformity on the arts remains in the background of Istina's narrative. In Janet Frame's autobiography, however, the struggle to claim an artistic vocation moves to the forefront. Henke compares Frame with Stephen Dedalus, the protagonist of James Joyce's *A Portrait of the Artist as a Young Man*; according to Henke, both "are fiercely independent, perpetually marginal and always seeking a private place/space that will define them as artists."[47] Frame's frustrated desire to be a writer results in a suicide attempt and her first hospitalization. Her decision to kill herself stems from the necessity of having to return to a teaching job that is stifling her. "I was forced to realize that suicide was my only escape," she writes.

> What, *in all the world,* could I do to earn my living and still live as myself, as I knew myself to be. Temporary masks, I knew, had their place; everyone was wearing them, they were the human rage; but not masks cemented in place until the wearer could not breathe and was eventually suffocated.[48]

The suffocation Frame feels as a teacher recalls an earlier part in her autobiography, in which she describes a time she wrote in her diary, *"They think I'm going to be a schoolteacher, but I'm going to be a poet."*[49]

After she is incarcerated, Frame grieves her many losses. "All I had left," she writes, "was my desire to be a writer, to explore thoughts and images which were frowned on as being bizarre, and my ambition, thought to be suspect, perhaps a delusion."[50] According to Frame, "Everyone felt that it was better for me to be 'normal' and not have fancy intellectual notions about being a writer, that it was better for me to be out of hospital, working at an ordinary occupation. . . ."[51] In addition, she knows that the desire to write does not necessarily indicate writing talent.

> Might I not, after all, be deluding myself like other patients I had seen in hospital, one in particular, a harmless young woman who quietly sat in the admission ward day after day writing her "book" because she wanted to be a writer, and her book, on examination, revealing pages and pages of pencilled 0–0–0–0–0–0–0–0.[52]

When she finally leaves the hospital, she is haunted by the thought that if there had been a way for her to write eight years earlier, she might have avoided hospitalization.

Ironically, Frame's desire to be a poet indirectly results in her hospitalization, and her enjoyment of language even contributes to her diagnosis. When she describes the gorse as having a "peanut-buttery smell," the doctor who read patients' letters determined that the phrase was an indication of schizophrenia; in actuality, Frame was quoting Virginia Woolf.[53] Eventually, however, Frame is saved by her artistic accomplishments, as is apparent from the incident that was the basis for the scene in *Faces in the Water* in which Istina is removed from the lobotomy list. According to Frame's autobiography, the superintendent of the hospital approached her with a newspaper in his hand. When she asked him what he thought about the operation, he replied, " 'I've decided that you should stay as you are. I don't want you changed.' "[54] Then he showed her the newspaper and informed her that her book *The Lagoon and Other Stories* had won the Hubert Church Award. She was taken off the lobotomy list, transferred to a better ward, and eventually discharged from the hospital.

Clearly, Frame's commitment cannot be attributed merely to her desire to write. Her struggle to realize her artistic vocation has many factors; she is not simply an alienated artist. The barriers for Frame include her sex, her lack of a privileged education, the economic situation of her family, and her nationality. "As a female artist," writes Henke, "Frame faced problems that the young Stephen Dedalus never envisioned."[55] According to Susan Ash, "Social expectations continue to generate a particular self-awareness about the fact of a woman writing," and Frame's autobiography "reads as if its narrator is very much aware that society still censures certain choices made by women, including the choice to write."[56]

Because she is willing to do almost anything to be viewed as an artist, Frame at first accepts her diagnosis of schizophrenia as a way of identifying herself as a creative genius. "As a very young woman growing up in rural New Zealand, she was offered a limited number of career or life paths," writes Gina Mercer. "For a creative woman at this time there was really nothing available apart from the construct of 'madwoman/genius.' "[57] Diane Caney argues that Frame's psychology teacher,

John Forrest, "almost coaxed the young woman into believing that madness and genius were inseparable and that schizophrenia was an asset to the serious poet."[58] Forrest's point of view, which Frame accepted for a period of time, equates madness and creativity in a manner that *Faces in the Water* resists. "In a desperate bid to maintain her sense of self and difference," writes Mercer, "she adopted this construct, only to find herself locked into it, with little opportunity for escape."[59] Frame is seduced by the attention she receives from Forrest, his romantic view of schizophrenia, and her desire to see herself as a writer. As Jennifer Lawn writes, Frame's autobiography "recounts, with bleak humour, the seductiveness of Romantic representations of madness and the personal influence of John Forrest."[60]

Frame's autobiography illustrates her struggle to find, both literally and figuratively, a room of her own. She is able to write because of the support of New Zealand writer Frank Sargeson and governmental assistance in her own country, and by literary grants, which she uses to travel overseas. She also accepts a disability pension for a time during her stay in England. Her motivation for traveling has more to do with avoiding hospitalization than with an acceptance of the cultural hegemony of England and the European continent. "At the suggestion of Frank Sargeson I applied for a Literary Fund grant to travel overseas," she writes. "I knew, and others knew, that leaving the country was my last hope to avoid life-long confinement in hospital."[61]

It is ironic that Frame received support from the British government on the basis of her history of mental illness, for Britain's cultural dominance is part of the reason she could not identify herself as a writer. New Zealand literature was not included in the canon of great literature; for a long time, Frame did not know the work of New Zealand writers.

> As a child I had looked on New Zealand literature as the province of my mother, and when I longed for my surroundings . . . to waken to imaginative life, all I could do was populate them with characters and dreams from the poetic world of another hemisphere and with my own imaginings. There was such a creation as New Zealand literature; I chose to ignore it, and indeed was scarcely aware of it. Few people spoke of it, as if it were a shameful disease.[62]

Even after Frame was established as a writer, her art continued to be influenced by the cultural hegemony of the United States and Great Britain. In "Departures and Returns," she describes how the editors of American and British publications would change the language of New Zealand writers, "often destroying both the meaning and the rhythm of the sentence."

> This absorption, even within one's own country, of another culture means a form of imprisonment for able-bodied words which languish and could die exiled from literature, never having the opportunity to work within it and enrich it. How much more magnified this imprisonment and exile may be in a world-setting, when countries high in literacy and publishing opportunities, reinforced by an abundance of exported films, can almost vacuum-clean, overnight, another culture and language.

Speaking specifically as a New Zealand novelist, Frame says, "We want our words." [63]

Frame's career as a writer was influenced by her nationality, her sex, and her socioeconomic status. However, the questions of power that are most clearly brought into focus in her autobiography concern psychiatric practice. She writes about a friend who was not saved from the lobotomy list. "My friend Nola, who unfortunately had not won a prize, whose name did not appear in the newspaper, had her leucotomy and was returned to the hospital," writes Frame. "The legacy of her dehumanizing change remains no doubt with all those who knew her; I have it with me always."[64] Frame views lobotomy as the "convenience treatment" of the era before medication. Although it is not clear whether she would also consider drugs to be a convenience treatment, Frame knows that non-treatment-related variables influence psychiatric practice. She won a literary prize and avoided a lobotomy; Nola was not so fortunate. Her name did not appear in the newspaper, so it remained on the lobotomy list.

Despite her analysis of psychiatric power, Frame appears to be unable to abandon completely the disease model of mental illness. She insists that she was never ill. "I had seen enough of schizophrenia to know that I had never suffered from it,"[65] she writes, and, indeed, the diagnosis is eventually determined to have been a mistake. Although she rejects the validity of the schizophrenia label, she knows she that she cannot fight it; "the weight of the 'experts' and the 'world' " are against her opinion.[66] Years later, doctors in London would subject her to a battery of diagnostic tests and decide that she was never schizophrenic. One of the doctors decided that she was suffering from the effects of her years of hospitalization; he also arranged for a National Assistance weekly payment so that she could write without other demands. He agreed with Frame that writing was a *need* for her, and he encouraged her to write the account of her hospital experiences that became *Faces in the Water*.

Although the doctors' pronouncement vindicates her own perceptions, it also takes away the identity that had become both a trap and a refuge. "Oh why had they robbed me of my schizophrenia which had been the answer to all my misgivings about myself?" she asks.[67] She compares the removal of her diagnosis to the stripping away of a garment she had worn for twelve or thirteen years, and she grieves its loss:

> I remembered how wonderingly, fearfully I had tried to pronounce the word when I first learned of the diagnosis, how I had searched for it in psychology books and medical dictionaries, and how, at first disbelievingly, then surrendering to the opinion of the "experts," I had accepted it, how in the midst of agony and terror of the acceptance I found unexpected warmth, comfort, protection: how I had longed to be rid of the opinion but was unwilling to part with it. And even when I did not wear it openly I always had it by for emergency, to put on quickly, for shelter from the cruel world. And now it was gone, not destroyed by me and my constant pleading for "the truth" allied to an unwillingness to lose so useful a protection, but banished officially by experts: I could never again turn to it for help.[68]

She leaves Maudsley Hospital "no longer dependent on my 'schizophrenia' for comfort and attention and help, but with myself as myself."[69]

Although Frame says she "disapproved of all psychiatric gods" and describes herself as "against psychiatry," she not only accepts the expert opinion of the London doctors but also uses it to assert that she was never schizophrenic. In 1975 *Commonwealth Miscellanies* published a letter that was written by Frame's former psychiatrist. The letter was supposedly forwarded to Victor Dupont, the editor of *Commonwealth Miscellanies*, by Frame herself. It reads, in part:

> Miss Janet Frame Clutha has told me that a number of literary scholars and editors of anthologies are publishing biographical comments which refer to her previous state of mind as sick or disordered. I understand that some people are going so far as to suggest that her creative ability is in some way related to a history of mental illness. . . . She has been seen by a number of eminent psychiatrists, all of whom agree with my opinion that she has never suffered from mental illness in any formal sense.

In addition, Dupont notes that "Any writer, the signer declares in conclusion, who publishes comments referring to her 'disordered mind' or 'Mental illness,' exposes himself to 'litigation.' "[70] Although she knows the power of the labeler, the detrimental effects of hospitalization, and the stigmatizing function of psychiatric diagnoses, Frame's insistence on the inaccuracy of her diagnosis indicates that she believes that there is a disease called schizophrenia. If she questioned schizophrenia as a category of disease, she would not have to maintain so strongly that she never suffered from it. Frame "provokes us into questioning fixed notions of madness or insanity," writes Russell. "In her determination to throw off the label of 'schizophrenia,' however, there is an implicit acceptance that this is genuine madness."[71]

After reading *Faces in the Water*, "we are encouraged to open rather than close the ending," as Ash writes. "We are encouraged to ask what constitutes the border between sanity and insanity, and to wonder what will happen to Istina."[72] Moreover, Frame's madness narratives support Laing's problematizing of the bifurcation of sanity and insanity. *Faces in the Water* and *An Autobiography* also illustrate that the strict enforcement of consensual reality and social conformity can cause "madness" by stifling individual expression. "[Laing's] thoughts on the way in which people respond as their essential selves to their own perception of reality and in turn the way in which this is interpreted and labelled," writes Jane Unsworth, "seems to correspond to the central theme of Frame's fictions." According to Unsworth,

> Frame presents a world in which interpretation of events and therefore the reality of individuals is entirely dependent on point-

of-view and consequently cannot be seen as objective. Indeed the world, and its occupants who consider themselves to be the guardians of "reality" as an objective absolute, stand on a ground of dishonesty and untruth. In employing elements of the supposed reality of her own experience in her fiction Frame is able to control and manipulate her narrative in order to force the reader to confront preconceived notions of objective reality very effectively.[73]

Through Istina's narrative in particular, Frame has remained faithful to the faces in the water, for she has indeed seen her own face among them.

Janet Frame's madness narratives offer a warning about what can happen to individuals when they are treated—or treat others—as if they are less than human. Although Frame writes mainly on behalf of people who are too often forgotten, she also fears for those who would forget that psychiatric patients are, indeed, people. "I ventured to hope for the quality of strength and vigilance in psychiatrists," she writes, "their continued examination and testing of their humanity without which they might become political operators infected with the endemic virus of psychiatry, politics, and some other professions—belief in the self as God."[74] In *A Question of Power*, Bessie Head portrays a society gone mad, in which members of the dominant class have taken on the role of sadistic gods and deny the humanity of the majority of the population.

Frame softens *Faces in the Water* to make the depiction of her experiences in New Zealand hospitals more acceptable and "credible." In the creation of Istina Mavet, she tried to make her protagonist "more credibly mad." She constructed the novel by

> recording faithfully every happening and the patients and the staff I had known, but borrowing from what I had observed among the patients to build a more credibly "mad" central character, Istina Mavet, the narrator. Also planning a subdued rather than a sensational record, I omitted much, aiming more for credibility than a challenge to me by those who might disbelieve my record.[75]

For Head, the evils of apartheid, rather than the terrors of madness and hospitalization, were difficult to represent in fiction. "I found the South African situation so evil," she writes, "that it was impossible for me to deal with, in creative terms."[76] It is not a matter of altering her portrayal for the sake of credibility or greater acceptance; the horror of life in South Africa stifles her.

A Question of Power tells the story of Head's fictional counterpart, Elizabeth, through third-person narration. The similarities between the two women suggest that the novel represents Head's reflections on her own life, particularly her periods of madness. Elizabeth's experiences correspond to many of the events of Head's life.[77] Elizabeth, like Bessie Head, is the child of a wealthy white woman and a black stable hand. Her father vanishes, and her mother is placed in a mental hospital, where Elizabeth is born. Her mother dies in the institution. Elizabeth is raised by a "coloured" woman, whom she believes to be her mother. When the woman's husband leaves her, she can no longer care for Elizabeth. The child is sent to a missionary school, where she learns the real story of her parentage. She also learns the legacy of her mother's "mad" act; she is constantly observed for signs of mental illness, and the other children quickly learn that Elizabeth will be blamed for every problem. " 'You must be very careful,' " the principle of the mission school tells Elizabeth when she arrives. " 'Your mother was insane. If you're not careful you'll get insane just like your mother.' "[78]

The alleged madness of Elizabeth's mother is defined by her failure to conform to the strict racial and class boundaries of apartheid South Africa. "What constitutes insanity in this case," writes Adetokunbo Pearse, "is the breaking of South Africa's Immorality Amendment Act of 1957."[79] To describe her mother's madness, the principal tells Elizabeth, " 'Your mother was a white woman. They had to lock her up, as she was having a child by the stable boy, who was a native.' "[80] No further explanation is necessary. Elizabeth learns later that her mother killed herself in the mental hospital, and, although one could argue that the suicide supports the claim that Elizabeth's mother was mentally ill, ample evidence to the contrary can be surmised from the circumstances. Elizabeth's mother was deprived of her lover, her child, and her freedom; she was labeled insane and confined to a mental hospital, her relationship denigrated as "madness." It is not hard to understand how Elizabeth's mother might have been driven to suicide.

Elizabeth eventually leaves South Africa, taking her son

with her, and lives as a refugee in Botswana. Most of *A Question of Power* takes place in Botswana, although the injustices of apartheid loom in the background throughout the book. Elizabeth's journey into madness results from the ideological madness of apartheid. Her madness fulfills her mother's legacy, but not in any kind of biological sense. Instead, Elizabeth is driven to madness by the loss of her biological mother and father, and by the oppressive conditions that caused their separation. Elizabeth struggles to make sense of an irrational world, in which the color of one's skin determines whether he or she will be treated as a human being. In *The Wretched of the Earth*, Frantz Fanon explores the connection between colonialism and mental disorders, and argues that identity is a central issue. According to Fanon,

> Because it is a systematic negation of the other person and a furious determination to deny the other person all attributes of humanity, colonialism forces the people it dominates to ask themselves the question constantly: "In reality, who am I?"[81]

Head might have decided to write an autobiographical novel as a way of both exploring her identity and understanding her experiences of madness.

Although *A Question of Power* depicts Elizabeth's journey through madness, it does not focus on categories of mental disease or the treatment of the mentally ill. In Head's novel, the questions of power are not directly related to madness. *A Question of Power* illustrates how a person's humanity can be ignored on the basis of race, sex, economic class, or nationality; in addition, the novel also depicts the particular vulnerability of women. Elizabeth's foster mother is economically dependent on a man who suddenly leaves her, and Elizabeth's husband has sexual relations with numerous women during their marriage. Elizabeth's refugee status in Botswana mirrors her loss of connection to any family member other than her son. As Huma Ibrahim points out, "Elizabeth suffers from a double exile, one which expelled her in no uncertain ways from the white world of her mother and the other from the black sociolinguistic tradition of her father."[82] During one of her visions, Elizabeth is accused of not being connected to the people because she doesn't know any African languages. Elizabeth is exiled from her family, her heritage, and her country, and, through her madness, she is even alienated from herself.

Because of the historical context of *A Question of Power*, madness is not represented as a form of oppression. As Megan Vaughn points out in *Curing Their Ills*, major differences exist between European discourses of madness and the construction of madness in colonial Africa. In Africa "the medical power/ knowledge complex was much less central to colonial control than it was in the modern European state." According to Vaughn, "the need to objectify and distance the 'Other' in the form of the madman or the leper, was less urgent in a situation in which every colonial person was in some sense, already 'Other.' "[83]

Furthermore, Vaughn states that the extent of institutionalization was different in colonial Africa than in Europe; she found no evidence of a "Great Confinement" parallel to what Foucault describes for Europe. According to Vaughn,

Whilst the history of insanity in Europe is the history of the definition of the mad as "Other," in colonial Africa the "Other" already existed in the form of the colonial subject, the African. The category of the mad African, then, more often included the colonial subject who was insufficiently "Other"—who spoke of being rich, of hearing voices through radio sets, of being powerful, who imitated the white man in dress and behaviour and who therefore threatened to disrupt the order of non-communication between ruler and ruled.[84]

Vaughn proposes that "The lunatic asylum cannot then be regarded as a major instrument of colonial social or political control."[85] *A Question of Power* supports Vaughn's thesis because Head's narrative primarily addresses racism and imperialism, which are among the controlling forces in southern Africa.

Following Vaughn's thesis, one could conclude that Head's mother is committed to an asylum for stepping out of her place. In South Africa, wealthy white women are not supposed to be intimate with black men, let alone a black man from a lower socioeconomic class. In a white supremacist society, however, the boundaries primarily apply to people of color. It is Head's father who steps out of his place in the social and racial order, and it is clear that his fate would have been very different. Head's mother is not incarcerated for failing to maintain the prescribed distance between herself and a racial "Other"; instead, her "madness" stems from contradicting the fundamental belief of apartheid—that persons of color are subhuman. The relationship between Head's mother and father is an affront to the system of racial separation. "To the South African government, Elizabeth's parents are moral as well as political criminals," writes Pearse. "To the [mother's] family, both mother and child are sources of social shame, and evidence of sexual depravity."[86] Head's mother's madness, then, is ideologically defined. For those who accept the ideology of apartheid, a sexual liaison between a wealthy white woman and poor black man can only be understood as madness. As Kathleen Flanagan writes, "gender, race, sexuality, and the dictates of society all commingle to establish a definition of sanity or insanity."[87]

To a certain extent, Elizabeth's madness can be understood in Laingian terms as a rational response to an irrational society. Apartheid depends on the ideology of white supremacy for its reasonableness; white supremacist discourses and practices are insane to anyone who affirms the full humanity of all people. As Head writes in a letter to Randolph Vigne, "a world based on complexion is an empty, and unimaginative world."[88] Unlike Frame and other writers of madness narratives, Head does not view madness as a crime or her incarceration as punishment; according to Head, her "crime" is her complexion.[89] "[W]hen Bessie Head, in *A Question of Power*, talks about madness, she is not only talking about her mother's madness, or for that matter her own," writes Ibrahim; "madness becomes a process requiring a rigorous analysis of the individual in a society which renders black and white relationships obsolete in inhuman ways."[90]

Elizabeth's madness takes a particularly theological direction. Head describes *A Question of Power* as "a private philosophical journey to the sources of evil."[91] In the novel, Elizabeth struggles with the problem of evil; her struggle could be defined in terms of theodicy, which is concerned with the role of God in human suffering. Given a world of widespread injustice, oppression, and suffering, which Head and her protagonist have faced personally, Elizabeth tries to understand the existence of evil. To frame the problem in theological terms, a theist must reconcile how a loving and omnipotent God could allow such evil and suffering in the world. The German theologian Dorothee Soelle has stated the question this way:

> how would you see God, the almighty powerful, supernatural being who is in heaven and could have stopped Auschwitz . . . and didn't do it—can you still deal with this God if that is *God*? I mean I don't think it is God, but some do. That's what I mean. How do these events change your own thought and concept of God? That's the deepest question of all of them.[92]

This question is particularly relevant to the situation in South Africa, in which the oppression of people of color has been justified theologically. Although, as Vaughn explains, colonialists viewed African peoples as biologically inferior, Christianity was also used to support white supremacy and the separation of the races. Though schooled in Christianity, Elizabeth does not profess to be a Christian and therefore does not have the same theological problems as Christian theists. Even when she looks for an otherworldly source for evil, she does not have to make her thoughts consistent with Christian theology. "It did not matter who had planned evil," Elizabeth decides relatively early in the narrative. "It was always there, the plan."[93] To Elizabeth, it seems that evil, rather than God, is omnipresent and eternal.

Because she knows the Christian scriptures, Elizabeth sometimes ponders biblical narratives as she tries to understand evil. For instance, she refers to the story of David and Uriah, in which David kills Uriah so that he can marry Uriah's wife, Bathsheba, who is pregnant with David's child. She quotes part of the narrative to illustrate the depths of human passion rather than the incomprehensible ways of God. According to Elizabeth, human passion is deeper than the plan:

> There seemed no safeguard against it, no nobility powerful enough to counter it, no depths to which the soul could not sink. . . . "David wrote a letter to Joab, *and sent it by the hand of Uriah*. And he wrote in the letter, saying, Set ye Uriah in the forefront of the hottest battle and retire ye from him, that he may be smitten, and die."[94]

Later Elizabeth asks,

> What is love?
> Who is God?
> If I cry, who will have compassion on me as my suffering is the suffering of others?
> This is the nature of evil. This is the nature of goodness.[95]

Her search for answers mainly takes place in hallucinatory dialogues with two male figures, Sello and Dan. The strong sexual component of Elizabeth's madness invites a psychoanalytic interpretation, but the sexuality in her visions can also be explained in theological terms. In Elizabeth's visions, sexuality is abusive or perverted. The sexual component of her visions can be interpreted to represent distorted relationships. Feminist theologians, such as Rosemary Radford Ruether, conceptualize sin as "the distortion of relationship, including relation to oneself." According to Ruether, "there is no evil that is not relational."[96] Colonialism in Africa distorted relationships at all levels, to the extent that even the relationship between people and the land has been damaged. Similarly, the images of effeminate male homosexuals in *A Question of Power*, images that are stereotypical and demeaning to gay men, probably also indicate a distortion of relationships. At the same time, the image of male effeminacy, as a symbol of weakness and submission, could also represent those Africans who collaborate with their oppressors.

Dan appears in Elizabeth's visions as a very powerful figure. As if to symbolize his power, Dan's "huge, towering black penis" is "always erected."[97] The image of Dan contains elements that feminist theologians have found in traditional Christian theology. Ruether and others have critiqued and rejected the worship of power, particularly male power, in the Christian tradition. Because of its insistence that God is male, orthodox Christianity can be accused of worshipping maleness.[98] The valorization of absolute power is also problematic. As Sharon Welch writes,

> The idea of an omnipotent and sovereign God . . . assumes that absolute power can be a good. In the Christian tradition, one does not attribute demonic or destructive traits to Deity. And yet absolute power *is* a destructive trait. It assumes that the ability to act re-

gardless of the response of others is a good rather than a sign of alienation from others.[99]

Elizabeth, like contemporary feminist theologians, rejects power-over-others in favor of power-with-others. Absolute power can be terrifying; as Sello tells Elizabeth, *"If the things of soul are really a question of power, then anyone in possession of power of the spirit could be Lucifer."*[100]

Bessie Head found certain aspects of African traditional religions to be far more credible than Christianity. She was profoundly impressed by John Mbiti's *African Religions and Philosophy;*[101] "from the first few pages," she writes, "he is my man."[102] Mbiti emphasizes the presence of the holy rather than the power of a distant God. Similarly, Head writes, "I simply want God in mankind instead of up in the sky."[103] In her novels, Head uses the word *God* "in a practical way":

> I cannot find a substitute word for all that is most holy but I have tried to deflect people's attention into offering to each other what they offer to an Unseen Being in the sky. When people are holy to each other, war will end, human suffering will end.[104]

Elizabeth also removes God from the heavens and recognizes the holiness of other people. "There is only one God and his name is Man," she says. "And Elizabeth is his prophet."[105] She answers the question that Soelle considers the "deepest of all of them":

> In spite of those three or four years of sustained nightmare, she really knew absolutely nothing, except that she had gained an insight into what the German concentration camps must have been like. The inmates had cried: "Oh Lord, where are you?" No lord had appeared to help them. No Lord ever would. She had no illusions left about God or mercy or pity. A victim simply stared in the face of evil, and died.[106]

Having rejected any god who would maintain, allow, or delay intervening in the evils of apartheid and colonial Africa, she embraces the human capacity for justice and love.

Elizabeth's recovery is not effected by psychological or medical intervention, and Joanne Chase even criticizes *A Question of Power* for its rejection of disease models of madness. Chase writes that "it seems a misrepresentation of the ordeal of the mentally ill to claim that it is creative and productive rather *than simply a sickness like any other.*"[107] Elizabeth's madness can be understood more readily in terms of conceptualizations of false consciousness than with the medical model of mental illness. She is "cured" by means of a philosophical and spiritual breakthrough. Elizabeth refers to Sello's rejection of absolute power and his affirmation of the mutuality of love as her "lever out of hell."[108] "Love is two people mutually feeding each other," Sello tells her, "not one living on the soul of the other like a ghoul."[109] Finally, Elizabeth knows that if an omnipotent God does not maintain the social order, then the questions of power must be answered by human action. Following these realizations, Elizabeth ceases to be a passive battleground for a struggle between good and evil. She can fully embrace her capacity for good and consequently participate in the creation of a just society. By concluding that the human community, rather than any deity, is responsible for social transformation, Elizabeth knows that there is both challenge and hope.

The ending of *A Question of Power* suggests that Elizabeth is no longer an exile. She reestablishes her connection to the land by placing one "soft hand" over it as "a gesture of belonging."[110] However, like *Faces in the Water*, *A Question of Power* does not end optimistically. Although Elizabeth has passed through madness, she still lives in a season of peril. The colonial powers have not been overthrown; racism, sexism, and classism continue to be pervasive. The madness narratives of Janet Frame and Bessie Head imply that it is not madness that should terrify us. The true dangers are oppressive social structures (including institutional psychiatry), distorted relationships between people, and the suppression of the imagination through social and ideological conformity. These are the hallmarks of our seasons of peril.

6

Epilogue: Listening to Women

Women's madness narratives constitute an important subgenre of women's autobiography. In addition to their historical and literary significance, these narratives raise important questions for U.S. social policy. Who is mad and who defines madness? How should we view "mental illness" and "mentally ill" persons? Is madness primarily an individual or social problem? What is society's responsibility to such persons? How can we prevent psychiatric labels from being used as the tools of xenophobia in general, and sexism, racism, and heterosexism in particular? How have "the politics of reality" (to use Marilyn Frye's phrase) stifled human creativity and the potential to imagine and create?[1]

Women's madness narratives pose these questions and help to clarify the issues that must be addressed. At the same time, autobiographical accounts of psychiatric treatment also illustrate the complexity of these issues. The present study shows that there are significant problems in the diagnosis and treatment of "mentally ill" women and offers additional support for the claims that psychiatric treatment is gender biased. Numerous incidents in women's madness narratives indicate that men set the norm for emotionally healthy behavior and that women are punished if they fail to conform to the prescriptions of their gender role. The issues involved in psychiatric care are not purely medical or psychological, and madness narratives raise the questions of power that are often obscured by psychiatric discourse.

The need to educate people about therapeutic practices, which was asserted by Ada Metcalf in the nineteenth century, continues to be a crucial matter. Realizing this need, Paula Caplan calls for a "demystification of the whole process" of psychiatric diagnosis. "Making the public aware of the way that *DSM* decisions are made is a powerful way to fortify both therapists and the general public against the negative effects such decisions can have," she writes. "This means looking at the shockingly unscientific basis of the *DSM*, the politics and arbitrariness involved in deciding who is normal, and the motives of the major players."[2] Women's madness narratives illustrate how psychiatric practice has served the interests of patriarchal society and helped maintain existing power structures. Indeed, Laura Brown asserts that feminist psychotherapy ought to be "a conscious and intentional act of radical social change, directed at those social arrangements in which oppressive imbalances of power hold sway."[3]

Although it is important to acknowledge the limits of literature's potential to contribute to social policy, women's madness narratives, by virtue of their autobiographical content, have an undeniably political function. As Sidonie Smith writes,

> autobiographical writing has played and continues to play a role in emancipatory politics. Autobiographical practices become occasions for restaging subjectivity, and autobiographical strategies become occasions for the staging of resistance.[4]

Unlike other literary forms, autobiography bears a strong resemblance to established forms of legal and political discourse. As firsthand accounts of psychiatric treatment, madness narratives can function as testimony or "eye-witness" reports; however, the truth claims of madness narratives, and of testimony in general, are not self-evident. As Joan Scott points out, "Experience is at once always already an interpretation *and* something that needs to be interpreted." According to Scott's analysis, the limits of experiential knowledge augment the political nature of experience. "What counts as experience," writes Scott, "is neither self-evident nor straight-forward; it is always contested and always therefore political."[5]

The testimony of persons who have been diagnosed as mentally ill is typically viewed with greater suspicion than other experiential accounts. As the case of Lydia Smith shows, a woman's psychiatric diagnosis can have an impact on the perceived credibility of her testimony. Psychiatric expertise is privileged over the experiential knowledge of mental patients, and psychiatric discourse, either directly or through its influence, serves to negate the truth claims of madness narratives. "Marginalized people," writes Sandra Harding,

> are thought to be the most irretrievably mired in their social situation; women, "natives," the poor, and other others are the models for the irrationality, social passions, immersion in the bodily, and the subjective against which dispassionate reason, social justice, historical progress, "civilization," and the objective pursuit of knowledge have been defined.[6]

The status of psychiatrists as rational scientists with expert knowledge allows their experiences and interpretations to be privileged over those of women mental patients, whose accounts are seen as irrational, emotional, and tainted by disease. Yet, the truth claims of psychiatrists are neither self-evident nor unbiased, and therefore are as subject to inquiry as the testimony of mental patients.

As the foregoing analysis of women's madness narratives has shown, no simple bifurcation exists between the perceptions of mental patients and those of psychiatrists. Historically, women's madness narratives reflect a variety of perspectives, and both critical and laudatory representations of psychiatric practice are found among recently published accounts. Furthermore, psychiatry itself is not uniform theoretically or in practice. The works of Szasz and Breggin, to use contemporary examples, are far more critical of psychiatric practice than are many of the madness narratives of the twentieth century. Although the multiplicity of perspectives must be acknowledged, it is crucial to consider the questions of power that not only shape these accounts but also influence their reception.

Madness narratives can be said to differ from legal testimony in the manner in which they narrativize experience. Testimony, particularly in courtroom proceedings, has the appearance of immediacy and spontaneity. Madness narratives, on the other hand, reflect the writers' craft and have an overall coherency that is typical of published accounts. In "The Value of Narrativity in the Representation of Reality," Hayden White argues that "real events" do not possess "the coherence, integrity, fullness, and closure" of "the stories we tell about imaginary life."[7] Therefore, the narrativizing of actual events, whether in the form of published histories (or autobiographies) or oral accounts (such as testimony or eye-witness reports), "impos[es] . . . the formal coherency that only stories possess."[8] According to White, narrativizing also imposes a moral meaning on events. Several of the women whose works are analyzed in this study explicitly viewed their narratives as tools for revolution or reform in the care of mental patients. The moralizing judgments contained in these madness narratives enhance their potential to provide the impetus for resistance, either as public policy reform or revolutionary action outside of sanctioned avenues for social change.

Throughout the history of psychiatric practice in the United States, social policy has had a tremendous impact on the treatment of those considered to be mentally ill. As Gerald Grob writes,

> public policy decisions at both the state and local level greatly affected patients, psychiatrists, and mental hospitals. Levies and sources of funding as well as differing structural and administrative systems also played a role in shaping the way in which the mentally ill would be treated.

According to Grob, "public policy often reflected professional and political concerns rather than patients' needs."[9] Decisions regarding the care of mental patients often stem from anything but altruistic motives. Grob sees the demise of the mental institution as another chapter in the failure to provide adequate care for persons diagnosed as mentally ill. "More than a century and a half after the creation of a system of public hospitals in the early nineteenth century," writes Grob, "American society had yet to resolve the pressing need for providing decent and humane *care* for its dependent mentally ill citizens."[10]

According to Andrew Scull, the motivating factors for deinstitutionalization were economic rather than therapeutic.[11] Because public hospitals are expensive to maintain, community treatment options may be seen as cost-effective alternatives to the burden of caring for mental patients. After being discharged, however, many former patients end up homeless and have to struggle to obtain the resources necessary for survival.[12] Patients are released from state hospitals only to become alienated vagabonds, still separated from others by the

stigma of mental illness. A form of ideological institutionalization continues after hospitalization. Former mental patients
remain invisible even though they are no longer locked away
from "normal" people. Marked by poverty, disfiguring side effects from medications, and aimlessness, discharged mental
patients are so alienated that other people do not see them.
They are, like faces in the water, ignored and quickly forgotten.

The resurgence of medical models of mental illness has
raised questions about individual freedom as well as psychiatric treatment. Kate Millett argues in *The Loony-Bin Trip* that
involuntary treatment has given the psychiatric establishment
ultimate power over the minds and bodies of others. Similarly,
Thomas Szasz questions whether forced treatment or involuntary hospitalization can be justified. As Szasz writes, "The
view that the body is a biological machine—at once explicit
and implicit in the practice of modern medicine—requires a
decision about who controls or, so to speak, owns the body."[13]
In the era of deinstitutionalization, it has become increasingly
common for "outpatients" to be court-ordered to receive medication. According to Szasz, drug therapies control patients and
function as "chemical strait jackets."[14] Szasz calls involuntary
hospitalization a "crime against humanity,"[15] and perhaps
only an insane society would support such power over others.
As we have seen, Head's *A Question of Power* reinforces the
view that societies and ideologies can be insane. Head's narrative calls for individuals and communities to become sane by
rejecting unjust social structures and oppressive ideologies.

In addition to problematizing the sexual and racial biases of
psychiatric diagnoses, there is also the question of what is lost
by our current methods of treatment. What if, for instance,
Janet Frame had not been saved from the lobotomy list? How
many creative people have avoided psychiatric treatment, and
how many have been destroyed by it? As Peter Breggin writes,

Many people who seem "crazy" by ordinary standards never get
labeled mentally ill. They not only stay out of hospitals, they become great creators or leaders—or eccentrics. Similarly, many
people who are put into mental hospitals actually suffer from personal and social problems that have little or nothing to do with
being irrational.[16]

Moreover, if one of the roles of the imagination is to bring about personal and social transformation, as Adrienne Rich has argued, then any restrictions on the use of the imagination can have far-reaching implications. According to Rich,

> if the imagination is to transcend and transform experience it has to question, to challenge, to conceive of alternatives, perhaps to the very life you are living at the moment. You have to be free to play around with the notion that day might be night, love might be hate; nothing can be too sacred for the imagination to turn into its opposite or to call experimentally by another name.[17]

By placing limits on the creative potential of the mind, psychiatric treatment enforces the status quo as well as social conformity. In stifling the imagination, psychiatric practice might even inhibit our ability to answer the questions about psychiatric treatment. Women's madness narratives can break the cycle by interrupting psychiatric discourse, problematizing current practices, and envisioning new ways of being.

The artistic imagination might also help to cure society's neglect of those labeled mentally ill. In her autobiography, Frame describes how her mother encouraged her (and her siblings) to see the world from an artist's perspective:

> When Mother talked of the present, . . . bringing her sense of wondrous contemplation to the ordinary world we knew, we listened, feeling the mystery and the magic. She had only to say of any commonplace object, "Look, kiddies, a stone" to fill that stone with a wonder as if it were a holy object.[18]

Often the "mentally ill" are looked upon and dismissed. Just like those who miss out on the wonder of simple objects like stones, it is possible to ignore the humanity of people by labeling them mentally ill. Perhaps what is needed is an increased sense of the holiness of those labeled mentally ill. With this in mind, I return to Ussher's affirmation of the necessity of listening to women, particularly mad women.

Several writers have asserted the importance of listening to individuals who are or have been labeled "mentally ill." The value of firsthand accounts of psychiatric treatment has been affirmed by historians, psychiatrists, feminists, policymakers, and self-identified "survivors" of institutionalized psychiatry.

As the foregoing analysis demonstrates, patients raise different issues and have different perspectives than doctors, family members, or concerned citizens. Among the many positive effects of the antipsychiatry movement is the growing recognition of the need to listen to individuals who have been labeled mentally ill. In January 2000, the National Council on Disability released a potentially groundbreaking document, *From Privileges to Rights: People Labeled with Psychiatric Disabilities Speak for Themselves*, which summarizes a hearing in which "persons with psychiatric disabilities" were the primary informants. According to the NCD report, "The testimony pointed to the inescapable fact that people with psychiatric disabilities are systematically and routinely deprived of their rights, and treated as less than full citizens or full human beings." [19]

The firsthand accounts included in the NCD report bear striking similarities to the madness narratives discussed in this study, particularly in regard to psychiatric abuse. As the report states,

> NCD heard testimony graphically describing how people with psychiatric disabilities have been beaten, shocked, isolated, incarcerated, restricted, raped, deprived of food and bathroom privileges, and physically and psychologically abused in institutions and in their communities.[20]

The NCD hearing also amassed evidence of the prevalence of forced treatment and the widespread overuse of psychoactive medication, and the report urges an end to coercive treatment. "People with psychiatric disabilities are the only Americans who can have their freedom taken away and be institutionalized or incarcerated without being convicted of a crime and with minimal or no respect for their due process rights," the report states.[21] Among the conclusions drawn by the NCD is that "the manner in which American society treats people with psychiatric disabilities constitutes a national emergency and a national disgrace."[22]

The basic assumption of the NCD report is that "people with psychiatric disabilities" must be allowed to participate in decisions that affect their care. According to the report, "one of the reasons public policy concerning psychiatric disability is so different from that concerning other disabilities is the systematic exclusion of people with psychiatric disabilities from policymaking." For the most part, psychiatric patients have not been part of the debates surrounding public policy decisions, and, as the present study has shown, some women wrote madness narratives so that their experiences might have a public hearing. Firsthand accounts of psychiatric treatment, whether written as madness narratives or presented as testimony before a public hearing, can restore an essential perspective—that of patients themselves—to the development of social policy.

In addition to their potential to inform decisions regarding public policy, madness narratives provide a framework for women to understand their experiences and can facilitate alliances between women, particularly those who reject the perspective of their doctors. Such affiliations can lead to collaborative advocacy efforts and provide mutual support, as is apparent from the friendship of Elizabeth Packard and Ada Metcalf. Madness narratives can create a space for dialogue among previously isolated women. Kate Millett describes a conversation with Jill Johnston that occurred before either woman had published her madness narrative. According to Millett, there was no common ground to talk about their experiences. "I describe my craziness and ask after hers. But hers is incomprehensible to me, I cannot imagine what it was like," writes Millett. "Jill understands my craziness no better than I understand hers."[23] Madness narratives can create bridges that are difficult to build in ordinary conversations, and the autobiographies of Millett and Johnston illustrate the many commonalities of their experiences.

It is clear from the narratives discussed in this study that the nature of the relationships between people are of critical importance. Labeling contributes to the power imbalance between doctor and patient, and interferes with the formation of supportive relationships. "The only reason to call [people] schizophrenic is to justify the psychiatric establishment and its treatments," writes Breggin. "By refusing to diagnose or to label people who already feel rejected and humiliated, we welcome them back to the human community and promote humane, respectful, and loving attitudes toward them."[24] We may be able to find better answers to the questions posed in this study by focusing on relations—both to other people and to larger social structures—rather than on the diagnosis and treatment of individuals. In acknowledging the psychological effects of oppression, "the emphasis would not be on compartmentalizing those effects but rather on detailing the diverse types of oppression, expanding on the different forms of this relation," writes Denise Russell.

> Just as the focus is not on the oppressed, on one side of the relation, so it is not on the oppressor, the other side of the relation. Rather, to focus on relations is to focus on structures, complex networks which people are caught in often unawares.

According to Russell, "We are what we are, with whatever problems we have, because of our connectedness to others."[25]

Women write madness narratives to understand themselves and to present their experiences to others. Although narratives are not a substitute for relationships, one way of listening to other women is to read their autobiographies. However, as the foregoing discussion shows, women's perceptions can be influenced by psychiatric discourse. The tremendous power imbalance between psychiatrists and hospitalized mental patients can lead women to accept their doctors' opinions, sometimes even without question. Psychiatric theories and diagnostic labels interfere with the ability to speak and listen effectively, and it is important to allow women to speak on their own terms. Truly listening to "mad" women requires not only being open to what they have to say but also allowing their narratives to shape the way that we view madness and psychiatric practice.

Notes

CHAPTER 1: WOMEN'S MADNESS NARRATIVES AND THE SENTENCE OF HISTORY

1. Homi K. Bhabha, *The Location of Culture* (New York: Routledge, 1994), 172.

2. Elizabeth Packard, *Modern Persecution or Insane Asylums Unveiled, Mental Illness and Social Policy: The American Experience*, 2 vols. (1875; reprint, 2 vols. in 1, New York: Arno, 1973); Ada Metcalf, *Lunatic Asylums: And How I Became an Inmate of One* (Ottaway, 1876); Clarissa Caldwell Lathrop, *A Secret Institution* (Bryant, 1890); and Lydia Smith, *Behind the Scenes; or, Life in an Insane Asylum* (Culver, 1879); these narratives are discussed in chapter 2. Jane Hillyer, *Reluctantly Told* (New York: Macmillan, 1926); Barbara Field Benziger, *The Prison of My Mind* (New York: Walker, 1969); and Joanne Greenberg, *I Never Promised You a Rose Garden* (New York: Signet-NAL, 1964); see chapter 3 for an analysis of these narratives. Kate Millett, *The Loony-Bin Trip* (New York: Simon, 1990); Jill Johnston, *Paper Daughter* (New York: Knopf, 1985); and Susanna Kaysen, *Girl, Interrupted* (New York: Random House, 1993); see chapter 4.

3. The era of exclusively physician-centered histories is past. Historians and literary scholars have turned to firsthand accounts of psychiatric treatment, as well as other nontraditional materials, as historical sources. See, for instance, Mary Elene Wood, *The Writing on the Wall* (Urbana: University of Illinois Press, 1994); and Roy Porter, *A Social History of Madness: The World through the Eyes of the Insane* (New York: Weidenfeld and Nicolson, 1988). Patients' experiences also have been an important resource for research in other disciplines. See, for example, Carol Warren's *Mad Wives: Schizophrenic Women in the 1950s* (New Brunswick, NJ: Rutgers University Press, 1987), a sociological study.

4. Jeffrey L. Geller and Maxine Harris, eds., *Women of the Asylum* (New York: Anchor-Doubleday, 1994) 326.

5. Roy Porter, "The Patient's View: Doing Medical History from Below," *Theory and Society* 14 (1985): 181.

6. Porter, *Social History of Madness*, 181.

7. Porter, "The Patient's View," 175.

8. Porter, "The Patient's View," 194.

9. Geller and Harris, *Women of the Asylum*, 6.

10. Porter, *Social History of Madness*, 36.

11. On Whig historiography, see Herbert Butterfield, *The Whig Interpretation of History* (London: Bell, 1931). Examples of "Whig" histories of psychiatry include Lowell S. Selling, *Men against Madness* (New York: Greenberg, 1940); Gregory Zilboorg (with the collaboration of George W. Henry), *A His-*

tory of Medical Psychiatry (New York: Norton, 1941); Walter Bromberg, *Man above Humanity* (Philadelphia: Lippincott, 1954); and Jan Ehrenwald, *From Medicine Man to Freud* (New York: Dell, 1957). For a discussion of these histories, see Mark S. Micale and Roy Porter, "Introduction: Reflections on Psychiatry and Its Histories," in *Discovering the History of Psychiatry*, ed. Mark S. Micale and Roy Porter (New York: Oxford University Press, 1994), 6.

12. Albert Deutsch, *The Mentally Ill in America* (Garden City, NY: Doubleday, 1937). Gerald Grob classifies *The Mentally Ill in America* as "traditional or liberal" history because Deutsch "upheld the *theory* of institutional practice" despite his criticism of the actual care of mental patients (Grob, *Mental Illness in American Society, 1875–1940* [Princeton: Princeton University Press, 1983], ix; his emphasis). According to Grob, Deutsch was sympathetic to the aims of psychiatric care even though he was not a psychiatrist.

13. Michel Foucault, *Histoire de la folie à l'âge classique* (Paris: Plon, 1961); David Rothman, *The Discovery of the Asylum: Social Order and Disorder in the New Republic* (Boston: Little, Brown, 1971); and Andrew Scull, *Museums of Madness: The Social Organization of Insanity in Nineteenth-Century England* (New York: St. Martin's, 1979).

14. A great deal of controversy surrounds the work of Foucault, Rothman, Scull, and other "revisionists." Examples of opposing views include Constance McGovern, "The Myths of Social Control and Custodial Oppression: Patterns of Psychiatric Medicine in Late Nineteenth-Century Institutions," *Journal of Social History* 20 (1986): 3–21; and Grob, "The History of the Asylum Revisited: Personal Reflections," in *Discovering the History of Psychiatry*, ed. Mark S. Micale and Roy Porter (New York: Oxford University Press, 1994), 260–81. See also Scull, "Madness and Segregative Control: The Rise of the Insane Asylum," *Social Problems* 24 (1977): 337–51, and "Humanitarianism or Control? Some Observations on the Historiography of Anglo-American Psychiatry," *Social Order/Mental Disorder: Anglo-American Psychiatry in Historical Perspective* (Berkeley: University of California Press, 1989), 31–53.

Debates regarding the fundamental nature of psychiatric care (i.e., benevolent treatment versus social control) have fostered a number of important historical studies, all of which attempt to avoid adherence to either "side" of the controversy. These studies include Anne Digby, *Madness, Morality, and Medicine: A Study of the York Retreat, 1796–1914* (Cambridge: Cambridge University Press, 1985); William F. Bynum, Roy Porter, and Michael Shepherd, eds., *The Anatomy of Madness: Essays in the History of Psychiatry*, 3 vols. (New York: Tavistock, 1985–88); Nancy Tomes, *A Generous Confidence: Thomas Story Kirkbride and the Art of Asylum-Keeping, 1840–1883* (New York: Cambridge University Press, 1984), and "Historical Perspectives on Women and Mental Illness," in *Women, Health, and Medicine in America: A Historical Handbook,* ed. Rima D. Apple (New York: Garland, 1990), 143–71; Ellen Dwyer, *Homes for the Mad: Life inside Two Nineteenth-Century Asylums* (New Brunswick, NJ: Rutgers University Press, 1987), and "A Historical Perspective," in *Sex Roles and Psychopathology,* ed. Cathy S. Widom (New York: Plenum, 1984), 19–48. Grob's work comprises the most substantial body of non- or antirevisionist histories of psychiatry. See, in particular, *Mental Institutions in America: Social Policy to 1875* (New York: Free Press, 1973); *Mental Illness in American Society, 1875–1940*; and *From Asylum to Community: Mental Health Policy in Modern America* (Princeton: Princeton University Press, 1991).

15. R. D. Laing, *The Divided Self* (London: Tavistock, 1959; reprint, Baltimore: Penguin, 1971), and *The Politics of Experience* (New York: Ballantine-Random House, 1967); David Cooper, *Psychiatry and Anti-Psychiatry* (New York: Ballantine-Random House, 1971); and the many works of Thomas Szasz, especially *The Myth of Mental Illness* (New York: Harper, 1961). See also Judi Chamberlin, *On Our Own: Patient-Controlled Alternatives to the Mental Health System* (New York: Hawthorn, 1978). For a contemporaneous critique of antipsychiatry, see Martin Roth, "Psychiatry and Its Critics," *British Journal of Psychiatry* 122 (1973): 373–78. On the history of the movement, see Norman Dain, "Critics and Dissenters: Reflections on 'Anti-Psychiatry' in the United States," *Journal of the History of the Behavioral Sciences* 25 (1989): 3–25, and "Psychiatry and Anti-Psychiatry in the United States," in *Discovering the History of Psychiatry*, ed. Mark S. Micale and Roy Porter (New York: Oxford University Press, 1994), 415–44.

16. Erving Goffman, *Asylums* (Garden City, NY: Doubleday, 1961).

17. Nancy Tomes, "Feminist Histories of Psychiatry," in *Discovering the History of Psychiatry*, ed. Mark S. Micale and Roy Porter (New York: Oxford University Press, 1994), 351. Tomes's essay contains an excellent overview of relevant feminist studies.

18. Kate Millett, *Sexual Politics* (New York: Doubleday, 1970; reprint, New York: Ballantine-Random House, 1978); Shulamith Firestone, *The Dialectic of Sex* (New York: Bantam, 1970); and Phyllis Chesler, *Women and Madness* (New York: Doubleday, 1972; reprint, New York: Avon, 1973).

19. Chesler, *Women and Madness*, 118.

20. Chesler, *Women and Madness*, 31.

21. Among the numerous works that address gender issues in diagnosis and treatment are Paula J. Caplan, *They Say You're Crazy* (Reading, MA: Addison, 1995), a critical analysis of the *Diagnostic and Statistical Manual of Mental Disorders*; and Laura S. Brown, *Subversive Dialogues: Theory in Feminist Therapy* (New York: Basic, 1994). Broader works on women and madness include Jane M. Ussher, *Women's Madness: Misogyny or Mental Illness?* (Amherst: University of Massachusetts Press, 1991); and Denise Russell, *Women, Madness, and Medicine* (Cambridge, MA: Polity, 1994).

22. Elaine Showalter, *The Female Malady* (New York: Pantheon, 1985).

23. Sandra M. Gilbert and Susan Gubar, *The Madwoman in the Attic* (New Haven: Yale University Press, 1979) and Marta Caminero-Santangelo, *The Madwoman Can't Speak* (Ithaca: Cornell University Press, 1998).

24. Although I am indebted to *The Writing on the Wall*, my study expands on Wood's research by discussing madness narratives that are outside the scope of Wood's book.

25. Dain, "Critics and Dissenters," 9.

26. Examples include Jeanine Grobe, ed., *Beyond Bedlam: Contemporary Women Psychiatric Survivors Speak Out* (Chicago: Third Side, 1995); and

149

Irit Shimrat, ed., *Call Me Crazy: Stories from the Mad Movement* (Vancouver: Press Gang, 1997), an anthology of writings by Canadian men and women. Madness narratives can also be found in collections of lesbian "coming out" stories, such as Julia Penelope Stanley and Susan Wolfe, eds., *The Coming Out Stories* (Watertown, MA: Persephone, 1980). Many women received psychiatric treatment, including involuntary hospitalization, because they identified themselves as lesbian.

27. Dale Petersen, ed., *A Mad People's History of Madness*, Contemporary Community Health Series (Pittsburgh, PA: University of Pittsburgh Press, 1982); and Geller and Harris.

28. Phyllis Chesler, foreword to *Women of the Asylum*, ed. Jeffrey L. Geller and Maxine Harris (New York: Anchor-Doubleday, 1994) xiii.

29. Wood, *Writing on the Wall*, 1.

30. Estelle C. Jelinek, *The Tradition of Women's Autobiography: From Antiquity to the Present* (Boston: Twayne, 1986), xii.

31. Porter, *Social History of Madness*, 39.

32. Millett, *Sexual Politics*, 31.

33. Ussher, *Women's Madness*, 10–11.

34. Frantz Fanon, *Black Skin, White Masks*, trans. Charles Lam Markmann (New York: Grove, 1967), and *The Wretched of the Earth*, trans. Constance Farrington (New York: Grove, 1963).

35. Fanon, *Black Skin*, 98.

36. Leslie Rebecca Bloom, *Under the Sign of Hope: Feminist Methodology and Narrative Interpretation* (Albany: State University of New York Press, 1998), 66–69.

37. Ussher, *Women's Madness*, 289.

38. Ussher, *Women's Madness*, 306.

39. Bloom, *Under the Sign of Hope*, 64.

40. Barbara Christian, "The Race for Theory," in *Contemporary Postcolonial Theory*, ed. Padmini Mongia (New York: Arnold, 1996), 149; her emphasis.

41. Christian, "The Race for Theory," 149.

42. Nawal El Saadawi, *The Nawal El Saadawi Reader* (London: Zed, 1997), 11.

43. Arun Mukherjee, "Whose Post-Colonialism and Whose Postmodernism?" *World Literature Written in English* 30, no. 2 (1990): 1–9.

44. Carole Boyce Davies, *Black Women, Writing and Identity* (London: Routledge, 1994), 85.

45. Julia Watson and Sidonie Smith, "De/Colonization and the Politics of Discourse in Women's Autobiographical Practices," in *De/Colonizing the Subject: The Politics of Gender in Women's Autobiography*, ed. Sidonie Smith and Julia Watson (Minneapolis: University of Minnesota Press, 1992), xv.

46. George Mora, "The Psychiatrist's Approach to the History of Psychiatry," in *Psychiatry and Its History*, ed. George Mora and Jeanne L. Brand (Springfield, IL: Thomas, 1970), 4–9.

47. Studies of cultural representations of madness include Sander L. Gilman, *Seeing the Insane* (1982; reprint, Lincoln: University of Nebraska Press,

1996) and *Difference and Pathology: Stereotypes of Sexuality, Race, and Madness* (Ithaca: Cornell University Press, 1985); Otto F. Wahl, *Media Madness: Public Images of Mental Illness* (New Brunswick, NJ: Rutgers University Press, 1995); and Michael Fleming, *Images of Madness: The Portrayal of Insanity in the Feature Film* (Rutherford, NJ: Fairleigh Dickinson University Press, 1985).

48. Janet Frame, *Faces in the Water* (New York: Braziller, 1980), and *An Autobiography*, 3 vols. in 1 (New York: Braziller, 1991).

49. Bessie Head, *A Question of Power* (London: Heinemann, 1974).

CHAPTER 2: WRITING AS REBELLION

1. J. Sanbourne Bockoven, *Moral Treatment in American Psychiatry* (New York: Springer, 1963), 12.

2. Bockoven, *Moral Treatment*, 12–13.

3. Bockoven, *Moral Treatment*, 33–34.

4. Michel Foucault, *Madness and Civilization*, trans. Richard Howard (New York: Vintage-Random House, 1965), 246.

5. Foucault, *Madness and Civilization*, 247.

6. Russell, *Women, Madness, and Medicine*, 17.

7. Foucault, *Madness and Civilization*, 250.

8. Russell, *Women, Madness, and Medicine*, 14.

9. Foucault, *Madness and Civilization*, 257.

10. Qtd. in Foucault, *Madness and Civilization*, 258.

11. Foucault, *Madness and Civilization*, 258.

12. Russell, *Women, Madness, and Medicine*, 15.

13. Rothman, *The Discovery of the Asylum*, rev. ed. (Boston: Little, Brown, 1990), 144.

14. Dwyer, *Homes for the Mad*, 16.

15. Rothman, *Discovery of the Asylum*, 144–45.

16. Rothman, *Discovery of the Asylum*, 144; Rothman's ellipses and emphasis.

17. Szasz, *The Manufacture of Madness* (New York: Harper, 1970), 139.

18. Szasz, *Manufacture of Madness*, 146.

19. Szasz, *Manufacture of Madness*, 143.

20. Szasz, *The Second Sin* (Garden City, NY: Anchor-Doubleday, 1973), 119.

21. Russell, *Women, Madness, and Medicine*, 12.

22. Pliny Earle, "The Curability of Insanity," *American Journal of Insanity* 33 (April 1877): 532.

23. Packard, *Great Disclosure of Spiritual Wickedness in High Places with an Appeal to the Government to Protect the Inalienable Rights of Married Women*, Women in America from Colonial Times to the Present (1865; reprint, New York: Arno, 1974), 55.

24. Dorothea Dix, "Memorial of D. L. Dix, Praying a Grant of Land for the Relief and Support of the Indigent Curable and Incurable Insane in the

United States," 1848; reprinted in *On Behalf of the Insane Poor*, Poverty, U.S.A. (New York: Arno, 1971), 7; her emphasis.

25. David Gollaher, *Voice for the Mad: The Life of Dorothea Dix* (New York: Free Press, 1995), 164.

26. Gollaher, *Voice for the Mad*, 164.

27. John Charles Bucknill, "Notes on Asylums for the Insane in America," *American Journal of Insanity* 33 (1876): 138.

28. Dwyer, *Homes for the Mad*, 19.

29. Rothman, *Discovery of the Asylum*, 142–43.

30. Rothman, *Discovery of the Asylum*, 142.

31. Rothman, *Discovery of the Asylum*, 142.

32. Jelinek, *Tradition of Women's Autobiography*, 72, 78.

33. Packard, *Modern Persecution* 1:v.

34. Packard, *Modern Persecution* 1:34.

35. Packard, *Modern Persecution* 1:95.

36. Packard, *Modern Persecution* 1:95.

37. Packard, *Modern Persecution* 1:94–95.

38. Szasz, *Manufacture of Madness*, 130.

39. Packard, *Modern Persecution* 2:392.

40. Packard, *Modern Persecution* 2:399.

41. Packard, *Modern Persecution* 1:399.

42. Packard, *Modern Persecution* 1:399.

43. Packard, *Modern Persecution* 1:115.

44. Wood, *Writing on the Wall*, 26.

45. Packard, *Modern Persecution* 1:119.

46. For a thorough discussion of Packard's activities, see Myra S. Himelhoch and Arthur H. Shaffer, "Elizabeth Packard: Nineteenth-Century Crusader for the Rights of Mental Patients," *Journal of American Studies* 13 (1979): 343–76. See also Barbara Sapinsley, *The Private War of Mrs. Packard* (New York: Paragon, 1991).

47. "Illinois Legislation Regarding Hospitals for the Insane," *American Journal of Insanity* 26 (1869): 205–6.

48. "Annual Meeting of the Association of Medical Superintendents of American Institutions for the Insane," *American Journal of Insanity* 20 (1863): 89–92.

49. "Proceedings of the Association of Medical Superintendents," *American Journal of Insanity* 30 (1873): 175–76.

50. Metcalf, *Lunatic Asylums*, 69.

51. Metcalf, *Lunatic Asylums*, 13.

52. Metcalf, *Lunatic Asylums*, 65.

53. Metcalf, *Lunatic Asylums*, 63; her emphasis.

54. Metcalf, *Lunatic Asylums*, 13.

55. Metcalf, *Lunatic Asylums*, 59; her emphasis.

56. Metcalf, *Lunatic Asylums*, 22, 62.

57. Metcalf, *Lunatic Asylums*, 4.

58. Metcalf, *Lunatic Asylums*, 4.

59. Metcalf, *Lunatic Asylums*, 5.

60. Packard, *Modern Persecution* 2:215.

61. Metcalf, *Lunatic Asylums*, 55.

62. Metcalf, *Lunatic Asylums*, 24.

63. Metcalf, *Lunatic Asylums*, 20.

64. Metcalf, *Lunatic Asylums*, 22.

65. Metcalf, *Lunatic Asylums*, 6.

66. Metcalf, *Lunatic Asylums*, 33.

67. Metcalf, *Lunatic Asylums*, 4–5.

68. Metcalf, *Lunatic Asylums*, 4.

69. L. Smith, *Behind the Scenes*, 166.

70. L. Smith, *Behind the Scenes*, 166.

71. L. Smith, *Behind the Scenes*, n.pag.

72. L. Smith, *Behind the Scenes*, n.pag.

73. L. Smith, *Behind the Scenes*, 2.

74. L. Smith, *Behind the Scenes*, 2.

75. "Restraint in British and American Insane Asylums," *American Journal of Insanity* 34 (1878): 515–16.

76. L. Smith, *Behind the Scenes*, 3.

77. L. Smith, *Behind the Scenes*, 3.

78. L. Smith, *Behind the Scenes*, 3.

79. L. Smith, *Behind the Scenes*, 4–5.

80. L. Smith, *Behind the Scenes*, 212–13.

81. L. Smith, *Behind the Scenes*, 225.

82. Rush McNair, *Medical Memoirs* (Kalamazoo, MI: N.p., 1938), 53.

83. "The Kalamazoo Asylum: In a General Way Its Affairs Are Found All Right," *Daily Gazette*, 15 April 1879, 1.

84. "The Kalamazoo Asylum," 1.

85. Lathrop, *Secret Institution*, 138.

86. Lathrop, *Secret Institution*, 181.

87. Dwyer, *Homes for the Mad*, 67.

88. Dwyer, *Homes for the Mad*, 176. See also L. A. Tourtellot, "Utica Asylum Investigation," *American Psychological Journal* 2 (1884): 31–40; and Orpheus Everts, "The American System of Public Provision for the Insane, and Despotism in Asylums," *American Journal of Insanity* 38 (1881): 113–39. Everts criticizes reformers (whom he calls "agitators"), politicians, and neurologists. "Professed neurologists and flippant neurospasts of the medical profession," writes Everts, "arrogating to themselves all knowledge of psychology and psychiatry, have, by sneers, innuendo, and direct assault upon the character and qualification of medical officers serving in American hospitals for the insane, done what they could do toward the disparagement of hospital reputation" (117–18).

89. S. Weir Mitchell, "Address before the Fiftieth Annual Meeting of the American Medico-Psychological Association," *Journal of Nervous and Mental Disease* 21 (1894): 413–73.

90. Edward C. Spitzka, "Reform in the Scientific Study of Psychiatry," *Journal of Nervous and Mental Disease* 5 (1878): 202–29.

91. Dwyer, *Homes for the Mad*, 24.

92. Lathrop, *Secret Institution*, 201.

93. Lathrop, *Secret Institution*, 201.

94. Dwyer, *Homes for the Mad*, 207.

95. Lathrop, *Secret Institution*, 215.

96. Lathrop, *Secret Institution*, 215.

97. Lathrop, *Secret Institution*, 212.

98. Dwyer, *Homes for the Mad*, 207.

99. Dwyer, *Homes for the Mad*, 27.

100. Lathrop, *Secret Institution*, 215. During this period, the employment of women physicians in asylums was a subject of intense debate. For a discussion of the controversy, see Constance M. McGovern, "Doctors or Ladies? Women Physicians in Psychiatric Institutions, 1872–1900," *Bulletin of the History of Medicine* 55 (1981): 88–107.

101. Lathrop, *Secret Institution*, 213; her emphasis.

102. Wood, *Writing on the Wall*, 171n.

103. Lathrop, *Secret Institution*, 326.

104. Lathrop, *Secret Institution*, 186; her emphasis.

105. Lathrop, *Secret Institution*, 181.

106. Jelinek, *Tradition of Women's Autobiography*, 72.

107. Jelinek, *Tradition of Women's Autobiography*, 78.

108. Anna Agnew, *From under a Cloud; or Personal Reminiscences of Insanity* (Clarke, 1886).

109. Agnew, *From under a Cloud*, 195.

110. Agnew, *From under a Cloud*, v-vi. S. Weir Mitchell also argues for better-trained nurses. See Mitchell, "Address," 425–26.

111. Agnew, *From under a Cloud*, 184.

112. Dwyer, *Homes for the Mad*, 27.

113. Margaret Starr, *Sane or Insane? or How I Regained Liberty* (Baltimore: Fosnot, 1904), 11.

114. Agnew, *From under a Cloud*, 66.

115. Rothman, *Discovery of the Asylum*, 15–16.

116. Agnew, *From under a Cloud*, 66.

117. Agnew, *From under a Cloud*, 67.

118. Agnew, *From under a Cloud*, iv.

119. Agnew, *From under a Cloud*, 150.

120. Agnew, *From under a Cloud*, 150.

121. Agnew, *From under a Cloud*, 152.

122. For example, see Brown, *Subversive Dialogues*, 27.

123. Starr, *Sane or Insane?*, 18.

124. Starr, *Sane or Insane?*, 19.

125. Starr, *Sane or Insane?*, 109.

126. Starr, *Sane or Insane?*, 109.

127. Starr, *Sane or Insane?*, 24.

128. Starr, *Sane or Insane?*, 62; her emphasis.

129. Starr, *Sane or Insane?*, 86.

130. Starr, *Sane or Insane?*, 86.

131. Starr, *Sane or Insane?*, 117.

132. Starr, *Sane or Insane?*, 121.

133. Starr, *Sane or Insane?*, 114.

CHAPTER 3: TESTIFYING AGAINST THEMSELVES

1. These designations for mechanical restraint devices can be found, among other places, in "Restraint in British and American Insane Asylums," *American Journal of Insanity* 34 (1878): 514–15.

2. Rose Netzorg Kerr, *One Hundred Years of Costumes in America* (Worcester, MA: Davis, 1951), 23.

3. Elinor Roth Nugent, "The Relationship of Fashion in Women's Dress to Selected Aspects of Social Change from 1850 to 1950" (Ph.D. diss., Louisiana State University, 1962), 217.

4. Nugent, "Relationship of Fashion," 92.

5. Gail Pheterson, "Alliances between Women: Overcoming Internalized Oppression and Internalized Domination," *Signs* 12 (1986): 149. Cf. Suzanne Lipsky, "Internalized Oppression," *Black Re-emergence* 2 (1977): 5–10; and Liz Margolies, Martha Becker, and Karla Jackson-Brewer, "Internalized Homophobia: Identifying and Treating the Oppressor Within," in *Lesbian Psychologies*, ed. the Boston Lesbian Psychologies Collective, 229–41 (Urbana: University of Illinois Press, 1987). Internalized oppression is equated with learned helplessness (and psychiatric "compliance") in the National Council on Disability's report *From Privileges to Rights: People Labeled with Psychiatric Disabilities Speak for Themselves* (Washington, DC: Government Printing Office, 2000), 11.

6. Pheterson, "Alliances between Women," 149.

7. Germaine Greer, *The Female Eunuch* (London: MacGibbon, 1970; reprint, New York: Bantam, 1972), 91; her emphasis.

8. Lipsky, "Internalized Oppression," 5.

9. Sylvia Plath, *The Bell Jar* (London: Heinemann, 1963; reprint, New York: Bantam, 1972).

10. Inge Broverman et al., "Sex Role Stereotypes and Clinical Judgments of Mental Health," *Journal of Consulting and Clinical Psychology* 34 (1970): 1–7.

11. Audre Lorde, *Sister Outsider* (Freedom, CA: Crossing, 1984), 102.

12. Lorde, *Sister Outsider*, 102.

13. Charlotte Perkins Gilman, *The Living of Charlotte Perkins Gilman* (New York: Appleton, 1935).

14. Tomes, "Historical Perspectives on Women and Mental Illness," 153.

15. Showalter, *Female Malady*, 136.

16. Showalter, *Female Malady*, 138.

17. C. Gilman, *The Living of Charlotte Perkins Gilman*, 95.

18. Showalter, *Female Malady*, 135.

19. Showalter, *Female Malady*, 123.

20. Suzanne Poirier, "The Weir Mitchell Rest Cure: Doctors and Patients," *Women's Studies* 10 (1983): 35.

21. Showalter, *Female Malady*, 138.

22. C. Gilman, *The Living of Charlotte Perkins Gilman*, 96.

23. C. Gilman, *The Living of Charlotte Perkins Gilman*, 96.

24. C. Gilman, *The Living of Charlotte Perkins Gilman*, 121.

25. C. Gilman, *The Living of Charlotte Perkins Gilman*, 121.

26. C. Gilman, *The Living of Charlotte Perkins Gilman*, 314.

27. C. Gilman, *The Living of Charlotte Perkins Gilman*, 314–15.

28. Peterson, *A Mad People's History of Madness*, 240.

29. Barbara Ehrenreich and Deirdre English, *For Her Own Good: 150 Years of the Experts' Advice to Women* (Garden City, NY: Anchor-Doubleday, 1978), 126.

30. Ehrenreich and English, *For Her Own Good*, 247.

31. "Autobiography of the Insane," *Journal of Psychological Medicine and Mental Pathology* 8 (1855): 338.

32. Wood, *Writing on the Wall*, 129.

33. According to John P. Gray, mental hygiene and physical hygiene are "practically inseparable." See Gray, "Mental Hygiene," *American Journal of Insanity* 34 (1878): 307. For a discussion of Meyer and the mental hygiene movement, see David J. Rothman, *Conscience and Convenience: The Asylum and Its Alternatives in Progressive America* (Boston: Little, Brown, 1980), 302–23.

34. Clifford Whittingham Beers, *A Mind That Found Itself: An Autobiography* (New York: Longmans, 1908).

35. Wood, *Writing on the Wall*, 125.

36. Dain, "Critics and Dissenters," 9.

37. Peterson, *A Mad People's History of Madness*, 162.

38. Porter, *Social History of Madness*, 195.

39. Porter, *Social History of Madness*, 194.

40. Adolf Meyer, preface to *The Recovery of Myself: A Patient's Experience in a Hospital for Mental Illness*, by Marian King (New Haven: Yale University Press, 1931), x.

41. King, *Recovery of Myself*, 53–54.

42. King, *Recovery of Myself*, 126–27.

43. King, *Recovery of Myself*, 95–96.

44. King, *Recovery of Myself*, 127.

45. Hillyer, *Reluctantly Told*, 28.

46. Hillyer, *Reluctantly Told*, 90.

47. Hillyer, *Reluctantly Told*, 91.

48. Hillyer, *Reluctantly Told*, 28.

49. Hillyer, *Reluctantly Told*, 68.

50. Hillyer, *Reluctantly Told*, 59.

51. Hillyer, *Reluctantly Told*, 48–49.

52. Hillyer, *Reluctantly Told*, 13, 83; her emphasis.

53. Hillyer, *Reluctantly Told*, 83.

54. Hillyer, *Reluctantly Told*, 172–73.

55. Lucy Freeman, *Fight against Fears* (New York: Crown, 1951).

56. Peterson, *A Mad People's History of Madness*, 284, 285.

57. Freeman, *Fight against Fears*, 141.

58. Freeman, *Fight against Fears*, 319.

59. Freeman, *Fight against Fears*, 320.

60. Freeman, *Fight against Fears*, 292.

61. Freeman, *Fight against Fears*, 313.

62. Freeman, *Fight against Fears*, 292.

63. Freeman, *Fight against Fears*, 317.

64. Lenore McCall, *Between Us and the Dark* (Philadelphia: Lippincott, 1947).

65. C. Charles Burlingame, foreword to *Between Us and the Dark*, by Lenore McCall (Philadelphia: Lippincott, 1947), x.

66. Burlingame, *Between Us and the Dark*, ix.

67. Benziger, *Prison of My Mind*, 14.

68. Benziger, *Prison of My Mind*, 133.

69. Benizger, *Prison of My Mind*, 14.

70. Benziger, *Prison of My Mind*, 6.

71. Benziger, *Prison of My Mind*, 18; her emphasis.

72. Benziger, *Prison of My Mind*, 9.

73. Benziger, *Prison of My Mind*, 8; my emphasis.

74. Benziger, *Prison of My Mind*, 18.

75. Benziger, *Prison of My Mind*, 10.

76. Benziger, *Prison of My Mind*, 167.

77. Marguerite Albert Sechehaye, *Reality Lost and Regained: Autobiography of a Schizophrenic Girl*, trans. Grace Rubin-Rabson (New York: Grune, 1951); Ludwig Binswanger, "The Case of Ellen West," trans. Werner M. Mendel and Joseph Lyons, in *Existence*, ed. Rollo May, Ernest Angel, and Henri F. Ellenberger (New York: Basic, 1958), 237–364.

78. Grace Rubin-Rabson, translator's preface to *Reality Lost and Regained: Autobiography of a Schizophrenic Girl*, by Marguerite Albert Sechehaye (New York: Grune, 1951), v.

79. Flora Rheta Schreiber, *Sybil* (New York: Warner, 1973; reprint, New York: Warner, 1974).

80. Corbett H. Thigpen, *The Three Faces of Eve* (New York: McGraw, 1957).

81. Chris Costner Sizemore and Elen Sain Pittillo, *I'm Eve* (Garden City, NY: Doubleday, 1977).

82. Sizemore, *I'm Eve*, n.pag.

83. Mikkel Borch-Jacobsen, "*Sybil*—The Making of a Disease: An Interview with Dr. Herbert Spiegel," *New York Review of Books* 24 April 1997, 60.

84. Kit Castle, *Katherine, It's Time: The Incredible True Story of the Multiple Personalities of Kit Castle* (New York: Avon, 1990); Jean Small Brinson, *Murderous Memories: One Woman's Hellish Battle to Save Herself* (Far Hills, NJ: New Horizon, 1994).

85. Borch-Jacobsen, "*Sybil*," 63.

86. Lara Jefferson, *These Are My Sisters* (Tulsa, OK: Vickers, 1947; reprint, Garden City, NY: Doubleday, 1974).

87. Jefferson, *These Are My Sisters*, n.pag.

88. Bert Kaplan, ed., *The Inner World of Mental Illness* (New York: Harper, 1964), 3.

89. Jack Vickers, introduction to Jefferson, *These Are My Sisters*, 7.

Chapter 4: Questioning Psychiatric Power

1. Mary Jane Ward, *The Snake Pit* (New York: Random House, 1946; reprint, New York: NAL, 1970).

2. Ward, *Snake Pit*, 3.

3. Ward, *Snake Pit*, 4.

4. Ward, *Snake Pit*, 255–56; her ellipsis.

5. Ward, *Snake Pit*, 255.

6. Ward, *Snake Pit*, 256.

7. Ward, *Snake Pit*, 109, 87.

8. Deutsch, *The Shame of the States* (New York: Harcourt, 1948), 85.

9. Deutsch, *Shame of the States*, 84.

10. Ward, *Snake Pit*, n.pag.; cf. Ward, 217.

11. Ward, *Snake Pit*, 216–17.

12. Ward, *Snake Pit*, 216.

13. Ward, *Snake Pit*, 39.

14. Ward, *Snake Pit*, 38.

15. Ward, *Snake Pit*, 43.

16. Ward, *Snake Pit*, 43.

17. Ward, *Snake Pit*, 51.

18. Ward, *Snake Pit*, 50–51.

19. Ward, *Snake Pit*, 50.

20. Ward, *Snake Pit*, 91.

21. Ward, *Snake Pit*, 93.

22. Ward, *Snake Pit*, 93–94.

23. Ward, *Snake Pit*, 95.

24. David L. Rosenhan, "On Being Sane in Insane Places," in *The Invented Reality*, ed. Paul Watzlawick (New York: Norton, 1984), 140.

25. R. D. Laing, *The Divided Self* (London: Tavistock, 1959; reprint, Baltimore: Penguin, 1971), 36; Laing's emphasis.

26. Qtd. in Laing, *The Politics of Experience* (New York: Ballantine-Random House, 1967), 106–7; Laing's emphasis.

27. Laing, *Politics of Experience*, 107.

28. Laing, *Politics of Experience*, 107; his emphasis.

29. Laing, *Politics of Experience*, 108.

30. Laing, *Politics of Experience*, 108.

31. Ward, *Snake Pit*, 139.

32. Ward, *Snake Pit*, 141; her ellipsis.

33. Ward, *Snake Pit*, 67.

34. Ward, *Snake Pit*, 34.

35. Ward, *Snake Pit*, 165.

36. Ward, *Snake Pit*, 168.

37. Ward, *Snake Pit*, 255.

38. Ward, *Snake Pit*, 277–78.

39. Szasz, *Cruel Compassion: Psychiatric Control of Society's Unwanted* (New York: Wiley, 1994), 114.

40. Szasz, *The Myth of Mental Illness*, rev. ed. (New York: Harper, 1974), 267.

41. Szasz, *Myth of Mental Illness*, 12.

42. Szasz, *Myth of Mental Illness*, 268.

43. Szasz, *Myth of Mental Illness*, 267.

44. Scull, *Decarceration: Community Treatment and the Deviant—A Radical View* (Englewood Cliffs, NJ: Prentice-Hall, 1977), 82.

45. Scull, *Decarceration*, 86.

46. Scull, *Decarceration*, 139.

47. Szasz, *Cruel Compassion*, 189.

48. Russell, *Women, Madness, and Medicine*, 1.

49. Brown, *Subversive Dialogues*, 130.

50. Paula J. Caplan, *They Say You're Crazy* (Reading, MA: Addison, 1995), 31.

51. Russell, *Women, Madness, and Medicine*, 1.

52. Russell, *Women, Madness, and Medicine*, 155.

53. Kaysen, *Girl, Interrupted*, 39.

54. Kaysen, *Girl, Interrupted*, 5.

55. Kaysen, *Girl, Interrupted*, 39.

56. Kaysen, *Girl, Interrupted*, 131, 150.

57. Kaysen, *Girl, Interrupted*, 158.

58. Kaysen, *Girl, Interrupted*, 116.

59. Kaysen, *Girl, Interrupted*, 151.

60. Kaysen, *Girl, Interrupted*, 151.

61. Kaysen, *Girl, Interrupted*, 15.

62. Kaysen, *Girl, Interrupted*, 42.

63. Kaysen, *Girl, Interrupted*, 92.

64. Russell, *Women, Madness, and Medicine*, 156.

65. Johnston, *Mother Bound* (New York: Knopf, 1983).

66. Johnston, *Paper Daughter*, 225.

67. Johnston, *Paper Daughter*, 177.

68. Johnston, *Paper Daughter*, 170, 161.

69. Johnston, *Gullibles Travels* (New York: Links, 1974), 255.

70. Johnston, *Gullibles Travels*, 247.

71. Johnston, *Gullibles Travels*, 247.

72. Johnston, *Paper Daughter*, 72–73; my emphasis.

73. Peter R. Breggin, *Toxic Psychiatry* (New York: St. Martin's, 1991), 44.

74. Johnston, *Paper Daughter*, 247.

75. Ussher, *Women's Madness*, 239.

76. Showalter, *Female Malady*, 246.

77. Showalter, *Female Malady*, 247.

78. Brown, *Subversive Dialogues*, 125.

79. Johnston, *Paper Daughter*, 67.

80. Johnston, *Paper Daughter*, 72.

81. Johnston, *Paper Daughter*, 58.

82. Johnston, "Write First, Then Live," in *Queer Representations: Reading Lives, Reading Culture*, ed. Martin Duberman (New York: New York University Press, 1997), 344; Johnston's emphasis.

83. Johnston, "Write First," 343.

84. Johnston "Write First," 344; her emphasis.

85. Johnston "Write First," 344.

86. Millett, *Flying* (New York: Ballantine-Random House, 1974), 101, 103; her emphasis.

87. Millett, *Flying*, 384.

88. Millett, *Sita* (New York: Ballantine, 1978).

89. Millett, *Sita*, 245.
90. Millett, *Flying*, 444.
91. Adrienne Rich, *On Lies, Secrets, and Silence* (New York: Norton, 1979), 199; her emphasis.
92. Millett, *Flying*, 629.
93. Millett, *Sita*, 266–67.
94. Millett, *Flying*, 225.
95. Millett, *Flying*, 13.
96. Millett, *Flying*, 7.
97. Millett, *Flying*, 129.
98. Millett, *Flying*, 120–21.
99. Millett, *Loony-Bin Trip*, 262.
100. Millett, *Loony-Bin Trip*, 248.
101. Millett, *Loony-Bin Trip*, 248.
102. Millett, *Loony-Bin Trip*, 248.
103. Millett, *Loony-Bin Trip*, 248.
104. Millett, *Loony-Bin Trip*, 314.
105. Millett, *Loony-Bin Trip*, 314–15.

CHAPTER 5: SEASONS OF PERIL

1. Frame, *Autobiography*, 194.
2. Vanessa Finney, "What Does 'Janet Frame' Mean?" *Journal of New Zealand Literature* 11 (1993): 199.
3. Suzette Henke, "A Portrait of the Artist as a Young Woman: Janet Frame's Autobiographies" *SPAN* 31 (1991): 92.
4. Frame, *Autobiography*, 392.
5. Simon Petch, "Speaking for Herselves: The Autobiographical Voices of Janet Frame," *Southerly* 54 (1994–95): 66.
6. Elizabeth Alley, "An Honest Record: An Interview with Janet Frame," *Landfall* 45 (1991): 155.
7. Alley, "An Honest Record," 161.
8. Frame, *Faces in the Water*, 10.
9. Frame, *Faces in the Water*, 9–10.
10. Frame, *Faces in the Water*, 10.
11. Frame, *Faces in the Water*, 85.
12. Frame, *Faces in the Water*, 37.
13. Frame, *Faces in the Water*, 154.
14. Frame, *Faces in the Water*, 95.
15. Frame, *Faces in the Water*, 94.
16. Frame, *Faces in the Water*, 95.
17. Frame, *Faces in the Water*, 72; her emphasis.
18. Frame, *Faces in the Water*, 113.
19. Frame, *Faces in the Water*, 74.
20. Frame, *Faces in the Water*, 72.
21. Frame, *Faces in the Water*, 98.
22. Frame, *Faces in the Water*, 98.

23. Frame, *Faces in the Water*, 23.
24. Frame, *Faces in the Water*, 15.
25. Frame, *Faces in the Water*, 99.
26. Frame, *Faces in the Water*, 87.
27. Frame, *Faces in the Water*, 36.
28. Frame, *Faces in the Water*, 23.
29. Frame, *Faces in the Water*, 65.
30. Frame, *Faces in the Water*, 161.
31. Frame, *Faces in the Water*, 179.
32. Frame, *Faces in the Water*, 214.
33. Frame, *Faces in the Water*, 218–19.
34. Frame, *Faces in the Water*, 217.
35. Frame, *Faces in the Water*, 216.
36. Frame, *Faces in the Water*, 218.
37. Frame, *Faces in the Water*, 219.
38. Frame, *Faces in the Water*, 206–7.
39. Frame, *Autobiography*, 221.
40. Frame, *Faces in the Water*, 150.
41. Frame, *Faces in the Water*, 107.
42. Susan Schwartz, "Dancing in the Asylum: The Uncanny Truth of the Madwoman in Janet Frame's Autobiographical Fiction" *Ariel* 27 (1996): 113.
43. Frame, *Faces in the Water*, 112.
44. Frame, *Faces in the Water*, 27.
45. Paulo Freire, *Pedagogy of the Oppressed*, trans. Myra Bergman Ramos (New York: Continuum, 1989), 28; his emphasis.
46. Frame, *Faces in the Water*, 183.
47. Henke, "Portrait of the Artist," 87.
48. Frame, *Autobiography*, 188; her emphasis.
49. Frame, *Autobiography*, 132; her emphasis.
50. Frame, *Autobiography*, 213.
51. Frame, *Autobiography*, 222.
52. Frame, *Autobiography*, 224.
53. Frame, *Autobiography*, 213.
54. Frame, *Autobiography*, 222.
55. Henke, "Portrait of the Artist," 88.
56. Susan Ash, " 'The Absolute, Distanced Image': Janet Frame's Autobiography," *Journal of New Zealand Literature* 11 (1993): 37.
57. Gina Mercer, " 'A Simple Everyday Glass': The Autobiographies of Janet Frame," *Journal of New Zealand Literature* 11 (1993): 43.
58. Diana Caney, "Janet Frame and *The Tempest*," *Journal of New Zealand Literature* 11 (1993): 157.
59. Mercer, " 'A Simple Everyday Glass,' " 43.
60. Jennifer Lawn, "Docile Bodies: Normalization and the Asylum in *Owls Do Cry*," *Journal of New Zealand Literature* 11 (1993): 184.
61. Frame, "Beginnings," *Landfall* 19 (1965): 46.
62. Frame, *Autobiography*, 192.
63. Frame, "Departures and Returns," in *Writers in East-West Encounter*, ed. Guy Amirthanayagam (London: Macmillan, 1982), 92.

64. Frame, *Autobiography*, 223.

65. Frame, *Autobiography*, 224.

66. Frame, *Autobiography*, 224.

67. Frame, *Autobiography*, 381.

68. Frame, *Autobiography*, 375.

69. Frame, *Autobiography*, 385.

70. Victor Dupont, "Janet Frame: Postscript," *Commonwealth Miscellanies* 1 (1975): 176.

71. Russell, *Women, Madness, and Medicine*, 147.

72. Ash, " 'The Absolute, Distanced Image,' " 35.

73. Jane Unsworth, "Why Does an Author Who Apparently Draws So Much on Autobiography Seem Committed to 'Alienating' the Reader?" in *The Uses of Autobiography*, ed. Julia Swindells (London: Taylor, 1995), 28.

74. Frame, *Autobiography*, 376.

75. Frame, *Autobiography*, 387.

76. Head, *A Woman Alone* (Portsmouth, NH: Heinemann, 1990), 67.

77. See *A Woman Alone*, especially 3–5, 77–79.

78. Head, *Question of Power*, 16.

79. Adetokundo Pearse, "Apartheid and Madness: Bessie Head's *A Question of Power*," *Kunapipi* 5 (1983): 82.

80. Head, *Question of Power*, 16.

81. Fanon, *Wretched of the Earth*, 250.

82. Huma Ibrahim, "The Autobiographical Content in the Works of South African Writers: The Personal and the Political," in *Biography East and West*, ed. Carol Ramelb (Honolulu: University of Hawaii Press, 1989), 124.

83. Megan Vaughn, *Curing Their Ills: Colonial Power and African Illness* (Stanford, CA: Stanford University Press, 1991), 10. Although Vaughn focuses on Central and East Africa, she also discusses Botswana.

84. Vaughn, *Curing Their Ills*, 101.

85. Vaughn, *Curing Their Ills*, 120.

86. Pearse, "Apartheid and Madness," 83.

87. Kathleen Flanagan, "Madness as Exile, Madness as Power: Bessie Head's *A Question of Power*," *MAWA Review* 7 (1992): 91.

88. Randolph Vigne, *A Gesture of Belonging: Letters from Bessie Head, 1965–1979* (Portsmouth, NH: Heinemann, 1991), 109.

89. Vigne, *Gesture of Belonging*, 105.

90. Ibrahim, *"Autobiographical Content,"* 122.

91. Head, *Woman Alone*, 69.

92. Harry James Cargas, "Interview with Dorothee Soelle," *Encounter* 49 (1988): 85; Soelle's emphasis.

93. Head, *Question of Power*, 34.

94. Head, *Question of Power*, 34; her ellipsis and emphasis.

95. Head, *Question of Power*, 70.

96. Rosemary Radford Ruether, *Sexism and God-Talk* (Boston: Beacon, 1983), 181.

97. Head, *Question of Power*, 128.

98. See Ruether, *Sexism and God-Talk*, 125–26.

99. Sharon D. Welch, *A Feminist Ethic of Risk* (Minneapolis, MN: Fortress, 1990), 111; her emphasis.

100. Head, *Question of Power*, 199; her emphasis.

101. John S. Mbiti, *African Religions and Philosophy* (London: Heinemann, 1969; reprint, Garden City, NY: Anchor-Doubleday, 1970).

102. Vigne, *Gesture of Belonging*, 101.

103. Vigne, *Gesture of Belonging*, 91.

104. Head, *Woman Alone*, 99.

105. Head, *Question of Power*, 206.

106. Head, *Question of Power*, 200.

107. Joanne Chase, "Bessie Head's *A Question of Power*: Romance or Rhetoric?" *ACLALS Bulletin* 6 (1982): 71; my emphasis.

108. Head, *Question of Power*, 198.

109. Head, *Question of Power*, 197.

110. Head, *Question of Power*, 206.

CHAPTER 6: EPILOGUE: LISTENING TO WOMEN

1. The phrase comes from Frye's book *The Politics of Reality* (Trumansburg, NY: Crossing, 1983).

2. Caplan, *They Say You're Crazy*, 31.

3. Brown, *Subversive Dialogues*, 30.

4. Sidonie Smith, *Subjectivity, Identity, and the Body: Women's Autobiographical Practices in the Twentieth Century* (Bloomington: Indiana University Press, 1993), 156–57.

5. Joan M. Scott "The Evidence of Experience," *Critical Inquiry* 17 (1991): 797; her emphasis.

6. Sandra Harding, "Subjectivity, Experience, and Knowledge: Rainbow Coalition Politics," in *Who Can Speak?* edited by Judith Roof and Robin Wiegman (Urbana: University of Illinois Press, 1995), 132.

7. Hayden White, "The Value of Narrativity in the Representation of Reality," *Critical Inquiry* 7 (1980): 27.

8. White, "Value of Narrativity," 23.

9. Grob, *Mental Illness in American Society*, xii.

10. Grob, *Mental Illness in American Society*, 321; his emphasis.

11. Scull, *Decarceration*, 135.

12. Scull, *Decarceration*, 1–2.

13. Szasz, *Insanity: The Idea and Its Consequences* (New York: Wiley, 1987), 30–31.

14. Szasz, "Some Observations on the Use of Tranquilizing Drugs," *Archives of Neurology and Psychiatry* 77 (1957): 88.

15. Szasz, *Myth of Mental Illness*, 268.

16. Breggin, *Toxic Psychiatry*, 44.

17. Rich, *On Lies, Secrets, and Silence*, 43.

18. Frame, *Autobiography*, 9.

19. *From Privileges to Rights*, 11.

20. *From Privileges to Rights*, 11.

21. *From Privileges to Rights*, 11.
22. *From Privileges to Rights*, 3.
23. Millett, *Flying*, 237.
24. Breggin, *Toxic Psychiatry*, 46.
25. Russell, *Women, Madness, and Medicine*, 157.

Bibliography

Agnew, Anna. *From under a Cloud; or Personal Reminiscences of Insanity.* Clarke, 1886.

Alley, Elizabeth. "An Honest Record: An Interview with Janet Frame." *Landfall* 45 (1991): 154–68.

"Annual Meeting of the Association of Medical Superintendents of American Institutions for the Insane." *American Journal of Insanity* 20 (1863): 89–92.

Ash, Susan. " 'The Absolute, Distanced Image': Janet Frame's Autobiography." *Journal of New Zealand Literature* 11 (1993): 21–40.

"Autobiography of the Insane." *Journal of Psychological Medicine and Mental Pathology* 8 (1855): 338–53.

Beers, Clifford Whittingham. *A Mind That Found Itself: An Autobiography.* New York: Longmans, 1908.

Benziger, Barbara Field. *The Prison of My Mind.* New York: Walker, 1969.

Bhabha, Homi K. *The Location of Culture.* New York: Routledge, 1994.

Binswanger, Ludwig. "The Case of Ellen West." Translated by Werner M. Mendel and Joseph Lyons. In *Existence,* edited by Rollo May, Ernest Angel, and Henri F. Ellenberger, 237–364. New York: Basic, 1958.

Bloom, Leslie Rebecca. *Under the Sign of Hope: Feminist Methodology and Narrative Interpretation.* Albany: State University of New York Press, 1998.

Bockoven, J. Sanbourne. *Moral Treatment in American Psychiatry.* New York: Springer, 1963.

Borch-Jacobsen, Mikkel. "*Sybil*—The Making of a Disease: An Interview with Dr. Herbert Spiegel." *New York Review of Books,* 24 April 1997, 60–64.

Breggin, Peter R. *Toxic Psychiatry.* New York: St. Martin's, 1991.

Brinson, Jean Small. *Murderous Memories: One Woman's Hellish Battle to Save Herself.* Far Hills, NJ: New Horizon, 1994.

Bromberg, Walter. *Man above Humanity.* Philadelphia: Lippincott, 1954.

Broverman, Inge, et al. "Sex Role Stereotypes and Clinical Judgments of Mental Health." *Journal of Consulting and Clinical Psychology* 34 (1970): 1–7.

Brown, Laura S. *Subversive Dialogues: Theory in Feminist Therapy.* New York: Basic, 1994.

Bucknill, John Charles. "Notes on Asylums for the Insane in America." *American Journal of Insanity* 33 (1876): 137–60.

Burlingame, C. Charles. Foreword to *Between Us and the Dark,* by Lenore McCall. Philadelphia: Lippincott, 1947.

Butterfield, Herbert. *The Whig Interpretation of History*. London: Bell, 1931.

Bynum, W. F., Roy Porter, and Michael Shepherd, eds. *The Anatomy of Madness: Essays in the History of Psychiatry*. 3 vols. London: Tavistock, 1985–88.

Caminero-Santangelo, Marta. *The Madwoman Can't Speak*. Ithaca: Cornell University Press, 1998.

Caney, Diana. "Janet Frame and *The Tempest*." *Journal of New Zealand Literature* 11 (1993): 152–71.

Caplan, Paula J. *They Say You're Crazy*. Reading, MA: Addison, 1995.

Cargas, Harry James. "Interview with Dorothee Soelle." *Encounter* 49 (1988): 123–28.

Castle, Kit. *Katherine, It's Time: The Incredible True Story of the Multiple Personalities of Kit Castle*. New York: Avon, 1990.

Chamberlin, Judi. *On Our Own: Patient-Controlled Alternatives to the Mental Health System*. New York: Hawthorn, 1978.

Chase, Joanne. "Bessie Head's *A Question of Power*: Romance or Rhetoric?" *ACLALS Bulletin* 6 (1982): 67–75.

Chesler, Phyllis. Foreword to *Women of the Asylum*, edited by Jeffrey L. Geller and Maxine Harris. New York: Anchor-Doubleday, 1994.

———. *Women and Madness*. New York: Doubleday, 1972. Reprint, New York: Avon, 1973.

Christian, Barbara. "The Race for Theory." In *Contemporary Postcolonial Theory*, edited by Padmini Mongia, 148–57. New York: Arnold, 1996.

Cooper, David. *Psychiatry and Anti-Psychiatry*. New York: Ballantine-Random House, 1971.

Dain, Norman. "Critics and Dissenters: Reflections on 'Anti-Psychiatry' in the United States." *Journal of the History of the Behavioral Sciences* 25 (1989): 3–25.

———. "Psychiatry and Anti-Psychiatry in the United States." In *Discovering the History of Psychiatry*, edited by Mark S. Micale and Roy Porter, 415–44. New York: Oxford University Press, 1994.

Davies, Carole Boyce. *Black Women, Writing and Identity*. London: Routledge, 1994.

Deutsch, Albert. *The Mentally Ill in America*. Garden City, NY: Doubleday, 1937.

———. *The Shame of the States*. New York: Harcourt, 1948.

Digby, Anne. *Madness, Morality, and Medicine: A Study of the York Retreat, 1796–1914*. Cambridge: Cambridge University Press, 1985.

Dix, Dorothea L. "Memorial of D. L. Dix, Praying a Grant of Land for the Relief and Support of the Indigent Curable and Incurable Insane in the United States." 1848. Reprinted in *On Behalf of the Insane Poor*. Poverty, U.S.A. New York: Arno, 1971.

Dupont, Victor. "Janet Frame: Postscript." *Commonwealth Miscellanies* 1 (1975): 175–76.

Dwyer, Ellen. "A Historical Perspective." In *Sex Roles and Psychopathology*, edited by Cathy S. Widom, 19–48. New York: Plenum, 1984.

———. *Homes for the Mad: Life inside Two Nineteenth-Century Asylums*. New Brunswick, NJ: Rutgers University Press, 1987.

Earle, Pliny. "The Curability of Insanity." *American Journal of Insanity* 33 (April 1877): 483–533.

Ehrenreich, Barbara, and Deirdre English. *For Her Own Good: 150 Years of the Experts' Advice to Women*. Garden City, NY: Anchor-Doubleday, 1978.

Ehrenwald, Jan. *From Medicine Man to Freud*. New York: Dell, 1957.

Everts, Orpheus. "The American System of Public Provision for the Insane, and Despotism in Asylums." *American Journal of Insanity* 38 (1881): 113–39.

Fanon, Frantz. *Black Skin, White Masks*. Translated by Charles Lam Markmann. New York: Grove, 1967.

———. *The Wretched of the Earth*. Translated by Constance Farrington. New York: Grove, 1963.

Finney, Vanessa. "What Does 'Janet Frame' Mean?" *Journal of New Zealand Literature* 11 (1993): 193–205.

Firestone, Shulamith. *The Dialectic of Sex*. New York: Bantam, 1970.

Flanagan, Kathleen. "Madness as Exile, Madness as Power: Bessie Head's *A Question of Power*." *MAWA Review* 7 (1992): 90–93.

Fleming, Michael. *Images of Madness: The Portrayal of Insanity in the Feature Film*. Rutherford, NJ: Fairleigh Dickinson University Press, 1985.

Foucault, Michel. *Madness and Civilization*. Translated by Richard Howard. New York: Vintage-Random House, 1965.

Frame, Janet. *An Autobiography*. 3 vols. in 1. New York: Braziller, 1991.

———. "Beginnings." *Landfall* 19 (1965): 40–47.

———. "Departures and Returns." In *Writers in East-West Encounter*, edited by Guy Amirthanayagam, 85–94. London: Macmillan, 1982.

———. *Faces in the Water*. New York: Braziller, 1980.

Freeman, Lucy. *Fight against Fears*. New York: Crown, 1951.

Freire, Paulo. *Pedagogy of the Oppressed*. Translated by Myra Bergman Ramos. New York: Continuum, 1989.

Frye, Marilyn. *The Politics of Reality*. Trumansburg, NY: Crossing, 1983.

Geller, Jeffrey L., and Maxine Harris, eds. *Women of the Asylum*. New York: Anchor-Doubleday, 1994.

Gilbert, Sandra M., and Susan Gubar. *The Madwoman in the Attic*. New Haven: Yale University Press, 1979.

Gilman, Charlotte Perkins. *The Living of Charlotte Perkins Gilman*. New York: Appleton, 1935.

Gilman, Sander L. *Difference and Pathology: Stereotypes of Sexuality, Race, and Madness*. Ithaca: Cornell University Press, 1985.

———. *Seeing the Insane*. 1982. Reprint, Lincoln: University of Nebraska Press, 1996.

Goffman, Erving. *Asylums*. Garden City, NY: Doubleday, 1961.

Gollaher, David. *Voice for the Mad: The Life of Dorothea Dix*. New York: Free Press, 1995.

Gray, John P. "Mental Hygiene." *American Journal of Insanity* 34 (1878): 307–41.

Greenberg, Joanne. *I Never Promised You a Rose Garden*. New York: Holt, 1964. Reprint, New York: Signet-NAL, n.d.

Greer, Germaine. *The Female Eunuch*. London: MacGibbon, 1970. Reprint, New York: Bantam, 1972.

Grob, Gerald N. *From Asylum to Community: Mental Health Policy in Modern America*. Princeton: Princeton University Press, 1991.

———. "The History of the Asylum Revisited: Personal Reflections." In *Discovering the History of Psychiatry*, edited by Mark S. Micale and Roy Porter, 260–81. New York: Oxford University Press, 1994.

———. *Mental Illness in American Society, 1875–1940*. Princeton: Princeton University Press, 1983.

———. *Mental Institutions in America: Social Policy to 1875*. New York: Free Press, 1973.

Grobe, Jeanine, ed. *Beyond Bedlam: Contemporary Women Psychiatric Survivors Speak Out*. Chicago: Third Side, 1995.

Harding, Sandra. "Subjectivity, Experience, and Knowledge: Rainbow Coalition Politics." In *Who Can Speak?*, edited by Judith Roof and Robin Wiegman, 120–36. Urbana: University of Illinois Press, 1995.

Head, Bessie. *A Question of Power*. London: Heinemann, 1974.

———. *A Woman Alone*. Portsmouth, NH: Heinemann, 1990.

Henke, Suzette. "A Portrait of the Artist as a Young Woman: Janet Frame's Autobiographies." *SPAN* 31 (1991): 85–94.

Hillyer, Jane. *Reluctantly Told*. New York: Macmillan, 1926.

Himelhoch, Myra S., and Arthur H. Shaffer. "Elizabeth Packard: Nineteenth-Century Crusader for the Rights of Mental Patients." *Journal of American Studies* 13 (1979): 343–76.

Ibrahim, Huma. "The Autobiographical Content in the Works of South African Writers: The Personal and the Political." In *Biography East and West*, edited by Carol Ramelb, 122–26. Honolulu: University of Hawaii Press, 1989.

"Illinois Legislation Regarding Hospitals for the Insane." *American Journal of Insanity* 26 (1869): 205–6.

Jefferson, Lara. *These Are My Sisters*. Tulsa, OK: Vickers, 1947. Reprint, Garden City, NY: Doubleday, 1974.

Jelinek, Estelle C. *The Tradition of Women's Autobiography: From Antiquity to the Present*. Boston: Twayne, 1986.

Johnston, Jill. *Gullibles Travels*. New York: Links, 1974.

———. *Mother Bound*. New York: Knopf, 1983.

———. *Paper Daughter*. New York: Knopf, 1985.

———. "Write First, Then Live." In *Queer Representations: Reading Lives, Reading Culture*, edited by Martin Duberman, 343–46. New York: New York University Press, 1997.

"The Kalamazoo Asylum: In a General Way Its Affairs Are Found All Right." *Daily Gazette*, 15 April 1879, 1.

Kaplan, Bert, ed. *The Inner World of Mental Illness*. New York: Harper, 1964.

Kaysen, Susanna. *Girl, Interrupted*. New York: Random House, 1993.

Kerr, Rose Netzorg. *One Hundred Years of Costumes in America*. Worcester, MA: Davis, 1951.

King, Marian. *The Recovery of Myself: A Patient's Experience in a Hospital for Mental Illness*. New Haven: Yale University Press, 1931.

Laing, R. D. *The Divided Self*. London: Tavistock: 1959. Reprint, Baltimore: Penguin, 1971.

———. *The Politics of Experience*. New York: Ballantine-Random House, 1967.

Lathrop, Clarissa Caldwell. *A Secret Institution*. Bryant, 1890.

Lawn, Jennifer. "Docile Bodies: Normalization and the Asylum in *Owls Do Cry*." *Journal of New Zealand Literature* 11 (1993): 178–87.

Lipsky, Suzanne. "Internalized Oppression." *Black Re-emergence* 2 (1977): 5–10.

Lorde, Audre. *Sister Outsider*. Freedom, CA: Crossing, 1984.

Margolies, Liz, Martha Becker, and Karla Jackson-Brewer. "Internalized Homophobia: Identifying and Treating the Oppressor Within." In *Lesbian Psychologies*, edited by the Boston Lesbian Psychologies Collective, 229–41. Urbana: University of Illinois Press, 1987.

Mbiti, John S. *African Religions and Philosophy*. London: Heinemann, 1969. Reprint, Garden City, NY: Anchor-Doubleday, 1970.

McCall, Lenore. *Between Us and the Dark*. Philadelphia: Lippincott, 1947.

McGovern, Constance. "Doctors or Ladies? Women Physicians in Psychiatric Institutions, 1872–1900." *Bulletin of the History of Medicine* 55 (1981): 88–107.

———. "The Myths of Social Control and Custodial Oppression: Patterns of Psychiatric Medicine in Late Nineteenth-Century Institutions." *Journal of Social History* 20 (1986): 3–21.

McNair, Rush. *Medical Memoirs*. Kalamazoo, MI: N.p., 1938.

Mercer, Gina. " 'A Simple Everyday Glass': The Autobiographies of Janet Frame." *Journal of New Zealand Literature* 11 (1993): 41–48.

Metcalf, Ada. *Lunatic Asylums: And How I Became an Inmate of One*. Ottaway, 1876.

Meyer, Adolf. Preface to *The Recovery of Myself: A Patient's Experience in a Hospital for Mental Illness*, by Marian King. New Haven: Yale University Press, 1931.

Micale, Mark S., and Roy Porter. "Introduction: Reflections on Psychiatry and Its Histories." In *Discovering the History of Psychiatry*, edited by

Mark S. Micale and Roy Porter, 3–36. New York: Oxford University Press, 1994.

Millett, Kate. *Flying*. New York: Ballantine-Random House, 1974.

———. *The Loony-Bin Trip*. New York: Simon, 1990.

———. *Sexual Politics*. New York: Doubleday, 1970. Reprint, New York: Ballantine-Random House, 1978.

———. *Sita*. New York: Ballantine, 1978.

Mitchell, S. Weir. "Address before the Fiftieth Annual Meeting of the American Medico-Psychological Association." *Journal of Nervous and Mental Disease* 21 (1894): 413–73.

Mora, George. "The Psychiatrist's Approach to the History of Psychiatry." In *Psychiatry and Its History*, edited by George Mora and Jeanne L. Brand, 3–25. Springfield, IL: Thomas, 1970.

Mukherjee, Arun. "Whose Post-Colonialism and Whose Postmodernism?" *World Literature Written in English* 30, no. 2 (1990): 1–9.

National Council on Disability. *From Privileges to Rights: People Labeled with Psychiatric Disabilities Speak for Themselves*. Washington, DC: Government Printing Office, 2000.

Packard, Elizabeth. *Great Disclosure of Spiritual Wickedness in High Places with an Appeal to the Government to Protect the Inalienable Rights of Married Women*. Women in America from Colonial Times to the Present. 1865. Reprint, New York: Arno, 1974.

———. *Modern Persecution or Insane Asylums Unveiled*. Mental Illness and Social Policy: The American Experience. 2 vols. 1875. Reprint (2 vols. in 1), New York: Arno, 1973.

Pearse, Adetokundo. "Apartheid and Madness: Bessie Head's *A Question of Power*." *Kunapipi* 5 (1983): 81–98.

Petch, Simon. "Speaking for Herselves: The Autobiographical Voices of Janet Frame." *Southerly* 54 (1994–95): 44–58.

Peterson, Dale, ed. *A Mad People's History of Madness*. Contemporary Community Health Series. Pittsburgh, PA: University of Pittsburgh Press, 1982.

Pheterson, Gail. "Alliances between Women: Overcoming Internalized Oppression and Internalized Domination." *Signs* 12 (1986): 146–60.

Plath, Sylvia. *The Bell Jar*. London: Heinemann, 1963. Reprint, New York: Bantam, 1972.

Poirier, Suzanne. "The Weir Mitchell Rest Cure: Doctors and Patients." *Women's Studies* 10 (1983): 15–40.

Porter, Roy. "The Patient's View: Doing Medical History from Below." *Theory and Society* 14 (1985): 175–98.

———. *A Social History of Madness: The World through the Eyes of the Insane*. New York: Weidenfeld, 1988.

"Proceedings of the Association of Medical Superintendents." *American Journal of Insanity* 30 (1873): 175–76.

"Restraint in British and American Insane Asylums." *American Journal of Insanity* 34 (1878): 512–30.

Rich, Adrienne. *On Lies, Secrets, and Silence.* New York: Norton, 1979.

Rosenhan, David L. "On Being Sane in Insane Places." In *The Invented Reality*, edited by Paul Watzlawick, 117–44. New York: Norton, 1984.

Roth, Martin. "Psychiatry and Its Critics." *British Journal of Psychiatry* 122 (1973): 373–78.

Rothman, David J. *Conscience and Convenience: The Asylum and Its Alternatives in Progressive America.* Boston: Little, Brown, 1980.

———. *The Discovery of the Asylum.* Rev. ed. Boston: Little, Brown, 1990.

Rubin-Rabson, Grace. Translator's preface to *Reality Lost and Regained: Autobiography of a Schizophrenic Girl*, by Marguerite Albert Sechehaye. New York: Grune, 1951.

Ruether, Rosemary Radford. *Sexism and God-Talk.* Boston: Beacon, 1983.

Russell, Denise. *Women, Madness, and Medicine.* Cambridge, MA: Polity, 1994.

El Saadawi, Nawal. *The Nawal El Saadawi Reader.* London: Zed, 1997.

Sapinsley, Barbara. *The Private War of Mrs. Packard.* New York: Paragon, 1991.

Schreiber, Flora Rheta. *Sybil.* New York: Warner, 1973 Reprint, New York: Warner, 1974.

Schwartz, Susan. "Dancing in the Asylum: The Uncanny Truth of the Madwoman in Janet Frame's Autobiographical Fiction." *Ariel* 27 (1996): 113–27.

Scott, Joan M. "The Evidence of Experience." *Critical Inquiry* 17 (1991): 773–97.

Scull, Andrew T. *Decarceration: Community Treatment and the Deviant—A Radical View.* Englewood Cliffs, NJ: Prentice-Hall, 1977.

———. "Madness and Segregative Control: The Rise of the Insane Asylum." *Social Problems* 24 (1977): 337–51.

———. *Museums of Madness: The Social Organization of Insanity in Nineteenth-Century England.* New York: St. Martin's, 1979.

———. *Social Order/Mental Disorder: Anglo-American Psychiatry in Historical Perspective.* Berkeley: University of California Press, 1989.

Sechehaye, Marguerite Albert. *Reality Lost and Regained: Autobiography of a Schizophrenic Girl.* Translated by Grace Rubin-Rabson. New York: Grune, 1951.

Selling, Lowell S. *Men against Madness.* New York: Greenberg, 1940.

Shimrat, Irit. *Call Me Crazy: Stories from the Mad Movement.* Vancouver: Press Gang, 1997.

Showalter, Elaine. *The Female Malady.* New York: Pantheon, 1985.

Sizemore, Chris Costner, and Elen Sain Pittillo. *I'm Eve.* Garden City, NY: Doubleday, 1977.

Smith, Lydia. *Behind the Scenes; or, Life in an Insane Asylum.* Culver, 1879.

Smith, Sidonie. *Subjectivity, Identity, and the Body: Women's Autobiographical Practices in the Twentieth Century.* Bloomington: Indiana University Press, 1993.

Spitzka, Edward C. "Reform in the Scientific Study of Psychiatry." *Journal of Nervous and Mental Disease* 5 (1878): 202–29.

Stanley, Julia Penelope, and Susan J. Wolfe, eds. *The Coming Out Stories.* Watertown, MA: Persephone, 1980.

Starr, Margaret. *Sane or Insane? or How I Regained Liberty.* Baltimore: Fosnot, 1904.

Szasz, Thomas. *Cruel Compassion: Psychiatric Control of Society's Unwanted.* New York: Wiley, 1994.

———. *Insanity: The Idea and Its Consequences.* New York: Wiley, 1987.

———. *The Manufacture of Madness.* New York: Harper, 1970.

———. *The Myth of Mental Illness.* Rev. ed. New York: Harper, 1974.

———. *The Second Sin.* Garden City, NY: Anchor-Doubleday, 1973.

———. "Some Observations on the Use of Tranquilizing Drugs." *Archives of Neurology and Psychiatry* 77 (1957): 86–92.

Thigpen, Corbett H. *The Three Faces of Eve.* New York: McGraw, 1957.

Tomes, Nancy. "Feminist Histories of Psychiatry." In *Discovering the History of Psychiatry,* edited by Mark S. Micale and Roy Porter, 348–83. New York: Oxford University Press, 1994.

———. *A Generous Confidence: Thomas Story Kirkbridge and the Art of Asylum-Keeping, 1840–1883.* New York: Cambridge University Press, 1984.

———. "Historical Perspectives on Women and Mental Illness." In *Women, Health, and Medicine in America: A Historical Handbook,* edited by Rima D. Apple, 143–71. New York: Garland, 1990.

Tourtellot, L. A. "Utica Asylum Investigation." *American Psychological Journal* 2 (1884): 31–40.

Unsworth, Jane. "Why Does an Author Who Apparently Draws So Much on Autobiography Seem Committed to 'Alienating' the Reader?" In *The Uses of Autobiography,* edited by Julia Swindells, 24–30. London: Taylor, 1995.

Ussher, Jane M. *Women's Madness: Misogyny or Mental Illness?* Amherst: University of Massachusetts Press, 1991.

Vaughn, Megan. *Curing Their Ills: Colonial Power and African Illness.* Stanford, CA: Stanford University Press, 1991.

Vickers, Jack. Introduction to *These Are My Sisters,* by Lara Jefferson. Tulsa, OK: Vickers, 1947. Reprint, Garden City, NY: Doubleday, 1974.

Vigne, Randolph. *A Gesture of Belonging: Letters from Bessie Head, 1965–1979.* Portsmouth, NH: Heinemann, 1991.

Wahl, Otto F. *Media Madness: Public Images of Mental Illness.* New Brunswick, NJ: Rutgers University Press, 1995.

Ward, Mary Jane. *The Snake Pit.* New York: Random House, 1946. Reprint, New York: NAL, 1970.

Warren, Carol. *Mad Wives: Schizophrenic Women in the 1950s.* New Brunswick, NJ: Rutgers University Press, 1987.

Watson, Julia, and Sidonie Smith. "De/Colonization and the Politics of Discourse in Women's Autobiographical Practices." In *De/Colonizing the Subject: The Politics of Gender in Women's Autobiography*, edited by Sidonie Smith and Julia Watson, xiii–xxxi. Minneapolis: University of Minnesota Press, 1992.

Welch, Sharon D. *A Feminist Ethic of Risk*. Minneapolis, MN: Fortress, 1990.

White, Hayden. "The Value of Narrativity in the Representation of Reality." *Critical Inquiry* 7 (1980): 5–27.

Wood, Mary Elene. *The Writing on the Wall*. Urbana: University of Illinois Press, 1994.

Zilboorg, Gregory, with the collaboration of George W. Henry. *A History of Medical Psychiatry*. New York: Norton, 1941.

Index